"Keep your thoughts positive because your thoughts become your words. Keep your words positive because your words become your behavior. Keep your behavior positive because your behavior becomes your habits. Keep your habits positive because your habits become your values. Keep your values positive because your values become your destiny."

MAHATMA GANDHI

FOREWORD

In 2007, the world was different. We were only six years removed from 9/11, and America was still trying to find its footing. Then came the financial crisis of 2008, commonly referred to as "The Great Recession." During that time, there were a lot of discussions about whether or not it was a good idea to start a company. There were two very distinct viewpoints: It was either an especially good time or an especially bad time, depending on who was making the argument. While some saw an unstable economy and a consumer-base more intent on saving than spending, others saw cheaper labor costs and reduced competition.

When I decided to launch TechStars, I wasn't weighing the pros and cons of whether or not 2007 was the best time to start a company. I simply saw a need in the Boulder startup community, so I went after it. TechStars has since become one of the largest tech accelerators in the world. The TechStars network has incubated hundreds of companies that have collectively raised over a billion dollars in venture capital and created thousands of jobs. In an environment categorized as catastrophic, TechStars—and its portfolio of companies—have thrived. So it's either always a good time to start a company, or always a bad time. Your choice.

The cornerstone of TechStars has always been its mentorship, and the strength of our network. Jesse was in the first class in 2007, and I'm glad he's part of the family. His book is full of insightful remarks, but the following quote might be the most telling. He says, "Simple truths are often the most elusive, overlooked, and forgotten."

Here's a simple truth that's core to Jesse's message: Our decisions make us who we are. The lines between success and failure, friendship and missed connection, happiness and unhappiness, barrier and breakthrough, are far thinner than we might imagine. Our mentality, and the decisions we make based on that mentality, play a huge role in our trajectory through life. Wherever *you* go in life, I hope you'll let the principles of the Connection Algorithm guide you.

David Cohen
TechStars Founder and CEO
November 2014

CONTENTS

STEP 2: COMMIT

STEP 3: CREATE

INTRODUCTION

"Whatever you can do, or dream you can, begin it.
Boldness has genius, power and magic in it."

JOHAN WOLFGANG VON GOETHE

I'm always amazed when I scroll through the contacts in my phone or my email account. Mixed in with family members and college friends are the names of high-profile CEOs, prominent venture capitalists, congressmen, and millionaires. I'm thirty-one years old. How did I do this? How did I build relationships with such powerful people at such a young age? Am I a genius? No. Do I have a special, God-given talent? No. Was I born into power and wealth? Not even close.

So, who is responsible? Should I thank the cofounder who took me on the wild ride of building a multi-million dollar company from the ground up? Should I thank the manager who introduced me to my cofounder? What about the VP who hired me to work at his thriving startup, or my most influential advisors and professors in college? How about my parents?

I am forever indebted to these people and I thank them often, both in my prayers and in person. They've undoubtedly contributed to my personal growth and good fortune. But there's an important underlying truth to consider: Although they've been instrumental in shaping my life, it has always been *my* decision to interact with them and learn from them. The relationships I've made, while integral to my development, are still a function of *my own choices*.

This realization is powerful. It means we don't need to possess a God-given talent or be born into wealth to do amazing things. We can simply expect to do amazing things and act accordingly. I've been doing this for most of my adult life without realizing it. This mindset, and the path that inevitably unfolds from it, is my gift to you. I call it the Connection Algorithm.

What This Book Is

The Connection Algorithm is the great idea that keeps you up at night. It's the hobby you can't ignore. It's the conference you've always wanted to attend. It's the blog post that changed your life. It's the investor who funded your project. It's curiosity, courage, failure, and success. In a word, the Connection Algorithm is a *mindset*, and this book will teach you how to harness it and use it to your advantage.

If you build this mindset into your life, it will accelerate your personal growth and naturally lead you to forge relationships with highly connected, successful people. It will also open your eyes to a new lifestyle, freeing you from the shackles of the 9-5 desk job. If this sounds too good to be true, it should. The doubt of the crowd affords opportunity to the few, which is precisely why the Connection Algorithm works.

You might find value in this book if:

- You're a young person who wants to accelerate your personal growth and education
- You're an entrepreneur dealing with challenging problems and want a better way to stay balanced and confident
- You want to build relationships with powerful people
- You want to become a leader, or hone your leadership skills
- You're tired of your boring job
- You've dreamt of following your passion, but can't seem to take the leap
- You aren't sure whether you should keep doing what you're doing or try something new
- You want to remove the chains of the 9-5 grind
- You want to be more productive
- You want to live a healthier life
- You want to overcome your fear of failure
- You want to squash self-doubt
- You want to live without regrets

What This Book Is Not

This is not a networking book. If you want to improve your networking skills, you've come to the wrong place. While making social connections is discussed briefly, you'll quickly come to realize that this book is primarily about making a connection with *yourself*. When your mind is conditioned properly, you'll develop an instinctive desire to explore, take risks, and connect. Building relationships is the last piece of the puzzle, and it's the least important. Your *mindset* is the engine that drives your behavior and everything that follows from it. It's the critical core that most people neglect.

This is not a self-help book. Self-help books are filled with rules and plans and lists designed to fix people's problems. The Connection Algorithm, although I define it as a formula, is not a formula for fixing problems. It is rather a broader way of thinking, which will change the way you navigate your world. *Self-help* implies you're in some kind of trouble, which would be pretentious of me to assume. Let's call it *self-enlightening* instead, meaning it will help you think more deeply about how you think. I consider this a lifestyle book. I invite you to internalize the concepts I present, but also to question them, test them, and form your own opinions about them.

This is not a get-rich-quick scheme. I will not be revealing the secret to getting rich quick. To the best of my knowledge, this only happens when playing the lottery or the Price is Right. My aim is to change your mindset so that getting rich quick becomes less of a concern—or no concern at all.

This is not a grand discovery. The concepts in this book are not new. Malcolm Gladwell discusses and defines Connectors in his acclaimed bestseller, *The Tipping Point*. Prominent bloggers and entrepreneurs like Tim Ferriss and Alexis Ohanian (among others) have outlined various tactics for building relationships. My purpose is to weave these commonly discussed topics into a new fabric—a fabric that specifically explores:

1. Risk-taking and relationship-building as vehicles for personal growth.
2. The mindset and behaviors required to maximize #1.

Too often, we assume that living our passions and connecting with our heroes is impossible. We assume it's a childhood fantasy—a dream. This book punches those assumptions in the face, and shows how *risk-taking* turns the dream into a reality.

Who I Am

I grew up in a small suburb outside of Washington DC. After surviving the public schooling system, I attended the University of Michigan, graduating four years later with a heap of debt and a flimsy certificate saying I wasn't dumb. Life after college was painfully dull. Two years after graduation, I was bored to death, working at a consulting firm in New York City. So, I quit my job and cofounded a startup, which went on to generate millions of dollars. I worked there for seven years, but I was eventually fired for being (admittedly) combative and generally useless. Battling intense fear and self-doubt, I picked myself back up again and decided to write this book.

I've taken a lot of risks in life, succeeded at a few things, and failed at many—but the world has never let me down.

ZombieLand

Do you feel safe? Comfortable? If your answer is "yes," I apologize in advance. I'm about to make you uneasy.

There's a good chance you're living in *ZombieLand*, where safety is just an illusion. ZombieLand is my term for institutionalized America—big business, public school, desk jobs, cable TV, and tabloid magazines. ZombieLand is anywhere you feel useless or uninterested in what you're doing. It's the status quo. It's where passion comes to die. Many of us assume ZombieLand is the safest place to build a career, but unfortunately, that type of stability is a thing of the past.

In ZombieLand, you sit at one desk. As a result, you learn very little. You tie yourself to a single company or a single skill and trust that you'll be able to sustain a comfortable living until you retire. The chances of this happening are slim to none. In today's workplace, the average worker switches jobs every four years. For recent grads, it's every *two* years. Job *instability* is the new normal.[3] It's not 1950 anymore, and the term *job security* has lost its luster.

To be frank, working in ZombieLand is the default choice—the lazy choice. It's going out of style as technology consumes all areas of the professional world. Tradesman are becoming obsolete, while experts, mavericks, and knowledge workers are becoming increasingly more valuable. Your ZombieLand security blanket isn't real. It's a relic from the past, and it could be ripped away from you at any moment. So why are you hiding under it in the first place? Acknowledging this false sense of security is the first step in looking beyond your cubicle and setting yourself free.

You might argue that joining the ranks of corporate America is more practical. Okay, I get it. The schooling system spits us out into ZombieLand. We're taught to graduate from college, throw our resumes at hiring managers, and settle into a desk job that best aligns with our degree. Practical? Yes. Effective in achieving the lifestyle you want? Not necessarily. I know too many people who hate their day-to-day routine (including my younger self).

Our society preaches that job stability correlates with happiness, but this isn't always the case. As our work culture evolves, this type of stability is becoming more and more correlated with settling, which often leads to boredom, which then leads to *unhappiness.* The Connection Algorithm seeks to deliver happiness through passion. It doesn't guarantee job stability, but it avoids boredom, which simultaneously enables great opportunity. If you feel stable but bored, there's good news: Rotting in ZombieLand isn't

---

3   http://tinyurl.com/ng5j2ot

the only option these days. New paths are emerging, fueled by startup accelerators, crowdfunding platforms, and the sharing economy. Today's breed of stability is built on bold decisions, adaptability, and unique experiences.

In the not-so-distant past, launching a business venture after graduation rarely crossed anyone's mind—and if it *did,* most people would shy away from it. *"That's too risky. How would I even get started?"* This play-it-safe, stand-in-line mentality is fading fast as the entrepreneurial ecosystem grows increasingly more robust. I'm not suggesting everyone should go build a business. It's actually incredibly difficult and most of us aren't cut out for it.[4] But that's okay. The key point is that rejecting ZombieLand is becoming more and more feasible—and lucrative.

The goal is not to work harder. The goal is to live the life you want to live, and to be in control. The goal is to eliminate the things that make you unhappy. For many of us—let's face it—that's our boring desk job. There has never been a better time in our country's history to make bold— even risky—career moves. With job security at an all-time low, you have little to lose, and a lot to gain. Don't use ZombieLand as a crutch or make it your default plan after graduation simply because it's staring you in the face. And if you're already in ZombieLand, don't trick yourself into thinking you can't leave. If you've ever dreamt of exploring your passions or doing something extraordinary, Zombie-Land is the very place you need to avoid.

---

4   *Business* is a broad term. In this case, I'm referring to a large organization with many employees, versus a one or two-person shop.

The Power of Connectors

We've all heard it: "It's not what you know, it's who you know." Like most expressions, this isn't entirely true in *every* situation, but most of us would agree that we can go further in life if we know powerful, well-connected people. Malcolm Gladwell, author of *The Tipping Point*, has a name for these people. He calls them Connectors. I'll be using the same term throughout this book, but with my own definition. I define Connectors as thought leaders, experts, and influencers in a given discipline, or range of disciplines. If you don't know any Connectors, your life probably looks something like this:

1. Go to school
2. Get a job
3. Try to get promoted
4. Try to find passion in whatever you're doing (even though you don't care that much)
5. Pay the bills on time and hope to save enough money for retirement
6. Continue steps 3-5 in perpetuity, realizing you'll never escape the cycle

Sound familiar? Let's be honest. This is the life most of us lead, and most of us wish we could change it. Luckily, Connectors can free us from this rut. They can surround us with intelligent people who will fuel our inspiration. They can help us launch new projects and companies. They can give us resources to learn, explore, and take risks. I know this because I've experienced it firsthand.

So, here's the question: If we agree that building relationships with Connectors can help us break free from the monotony of the corporate grind, and we agree that we aren't in love with the corporate grind, why don't we interact with Connectors and thrust open the doors of opportunity? For most of us, the cause for inaction is a little voice in our heads that says it can't be done.

We generally accept life as being prescribed to us. We abide by a set of arbitrary rules that are governed by an imaginary force. Somewhere along our journey of growing up, we begin interpreting these rules as Godly mandates and then blindly construct our lives around them. Here are some statements we generally accept to be true:

- School is the best place to learn.
- We should attend high school, college, and then graduate school, if we hope to do anything worthwhile.
- Creating a strong resume is the best way to get a job.
- Working our way up the corporate ladder is the best way to build a career.
- We should work between the hours of 9-5, five days a week.
- Vacation should be only a small respite from the time we spend working.

These statements are the manifestations of social constructs that were developed long ago to provide structure. But they are now the collective status quo—the cage we've built around our society—and for as long as we accept them, the cage will remain firmly intact. As you may have gleaned, I'm not a big fan of blindly accepting convention. It is often a recipe for mediocrity, limited thinking, and unhappiness. Although most people don't realize it, breaking free from these rules is as simple as deciding to do so.

You have the ability to do big things and build relationships with powerful people, regardless of where you started off on this planet, or where you are right now.[5] Your *decisions* most significantly determine your path through life—not your parent's zip code or the size of your noggin. When you consciously surround yourself with positivity, brilliance, and passion, your life will change dramatically. Both professionally and individually, you will become more capable than you ever thought possible.

Escaping ZombieLand takes work, but it's far more feasible than you think. You don't have to own a company or come from wealth, or be a genius or graduate from a top-rated school, or work countless hours at a demanding job. (In fact, you should avoid stressful jobs altogether.) There's no formula or list of steps that will guarantee your success and happiness, but there *are* a few core behaviors that will vastly improve your chances. It has little to do with innate talent. It has everything to do with relentlessly following your passions, being persistent, building a genuine support system, and knowing how to bend the rules of society to your advantage.

---

5   Think larger than life, like Warren Buffet, Oprah Winfrey, Barack Obama, Eric Schmidt. Although my aim is not for you to befriend a bunch of celebrities, it's important to think big.

The Beach, the Mountains, and the Swamp

In order to move forward, you have to know where you're starting from. Throughout life, you'll find yourself in one of three regions:

- The Beach
- The Mountains
- The Swamp

You'll travel through these regions multiple times. As you read the descriptions below, consider which region best describes your current situation.

The Swamp

People in the swamp are slogging through life. They dislike their day-to-day routine, but can't seem to alter it. They feel stuck.

If you're in the swamp (and it's easy to tell if you are—don't deny it), you *must* get out as quickly as possible. The swamp is a place of consistent unhappiness. It's important to realize that you won't somehow become happy without making drastic changes. Your subpar relationship will not suddenly become perfect. The boss you hate will not suddenly become fun to work with. Your mundane daily routine will not suddenly become exciting. Regardless of what you think you're working towards, you should jump ship. Given that you're currently unsatisfied with your surroundings, you *must* enter the mountains—for at least a little while—before heading to the beach.

The Mountains

If you're in the mountains, you're looking for excitement and happiness. You can climb incredibly high in this region, but it takes persistence. It's also dangerous—you could stumble and fall at any moment. On many occasions, you'll wish you had never started climbing, but then you'll finally reach a new peak and thank yourself for toughing it out. It's scary and difficult, but rewarding.

In the mountains, you're fighting for a better life.[6] While it can be stressful, it's the only way to gain control of your happiness if you don't already feel satisfied. Being in the mountains takes courage.[7]

The Beach

If you're at the beach, you're content. The beach is wide open. It's flat. Everything seems a little more simple and carefree. If you're in this region, you've probably already traveled through the mountains and the swamp. Some people find themselves at the beach and never venture out of it. I sometimes envy these people. But then I remember that the beach—while relaxing and beautiful—can also be painfully boring.

---

6   A *better life* means different things for different people. Be sure to define *better life* as it relates to *you* before chasing after it. Don't worry, this book will help you do that.

7   It's worth noting that it's possible, even common, to stay in the mountains forever and find happiness without ever experiencing the relaxation and bliss of the beach. Some people need the constant struggle to feel alive, and that's perfectly fine. So far, I'm this way. Maybe I'll settle at the beach eventually. But for now, I'm a climber.

If you're at the beach and you enjoy it, congratulations. You should be proud of the fact that you've found bliss. Just remember that happiness is a state of mind and not a final destination. You should constantly ask yourself whether you're as happy today as you were yesterday. If your happiness is slipping consistently over an extended period of time, you may want to venture into the mountains for a while.

A Final Thought on Boundaries

All three regions can be viewed in relation to boundaries. Beach residents are content with their boundaries, mountain residents are constantly challenging their boundaries, and swamp residents are discontent with their boundaries but do nothing to overcome them. We always face boundaries. Happiness is achieved through the acceptance of (not the surrender to) existing boundaries, or by continuously removing existing boundaries to uncover the next set.

Doing nothing to remove undesirable boundaries is the only fatal decision. Yet surprisingly, many of us live our lives this way. The swamp is synonymous with ZombieLand. You can't grow from a swamp. If you're in this region, you *must* find your way out. Be brave and confront your boundaries. The struggle is worth it.

The Four Cs

There are four overarching steps to escaping ZombieLand and accelerating your growth, which I call *The Four Cs*:

1. Choose
2. Commit
3. Create
4. Connect

1. Choose

You must first choose to take the leap. The leap represents your willingness to face your fears, risk failure, and push yourself beyond your own perceived limitations. It's the choice to leave ZombieLand. Before you leap, you must also decide what you're leaping toward. Are you planning to join your dream organization? Sell your own product? Invent something? Start your own company? Hold a public office? Start a movement? You have to decide where your passion lies. This could take some thought, or you may already know. The following chapters will help you either way.

2. Commit

After making the critical decision to leap, you need to commit. You need to go all in. The specifics of this step will vary significantly depending on your life situation and what you're trying to accomplish. The recent college grad is different from the single mother with two kids. But regardless of your specific scenario, you should commit as deeply as possible. You should remove all distractions, toss any crutches you might be leaning on, and ditch all backup plans. Don't set yourself up for failure, but realize you have to take chances and make sacrifices. Dipping your feet in the water won't cut it. At some point, you have to dive in.

Committing also means persisting. The best venture capitalists value persistence over intelligence when analyzing the characteristics of founders and CEOs. (Did you get that? You might want to read that last sentence again.) This is because crumbling under pressure is more likely to cause failure than an inability to solve problems. Persistence takes extreme mental toughness.

Here's a perspective from Ben Horowitz, an amazingly successful entrepreneur, writer, and venture capitalist:

> As CEO, there will be many times when you feel like quitting. I have seen CEOs try to cope with the stress by drinking heavily, checking out, and even quitting. In each case, the CEO had a marvelous rationalization about why it was okay for him to punk out or quit, but none of them will ever be great CEOs.
>
> Great CEOs face the pain. They deal with the sleepless nights, the cold sweats, and what my friend the great Alfred Chuang (legendary founder and CEO of BEA Systems) calls "the torture." Whenever I meet a successful CEO, I ask them how they did it. Mediocre CEOs point to their brilliant strategic moves or their intuitive business sense or a variety of other self-congratulatory explanations. The great CEOs tend to be remarkably consistent in their answers. They all say "I didn't quit."[8]

While this passage has particular relevance to entrepreneurs, it applies to everyone. If you have trouble relating to it, read it again, replacing *CEO* with *leader*. If you want

---

8   Ben Horowitz, *The Hard Thing About Hard Things*. (Harper Business, 2014).

to be the leader of your own life—and I hope you do—this applies to you.

If you're doing anything worthwhile, you'll want to quit at some point. You have to take that decision seriously. We'll discuss legitimate reasons for doing it, but you need to go into battle with the mindset that quitting is the last resort— something to be avoided at all costs. Face the fear. Lean in to the uncomfortable situations. If you never feel the urge to quit, you're not taking big enough risks.

3. Create

After choosing your path and committing to it, you must create something of value. This is arguably the most important step. Creating value doesn't necessarily require a tangible output, but your work needs to matter. If you're contributing to a project you truly believe in, you're creating value. If you're bringing people together around a shared belief, you're creating value. If you're changing people's lives for the better, you're creating value. Finding purpose, and driving positive change through that purpose, should be your goal. This book will teach you how to create value from your passions *with the lowest possible overhead.*

4. Connect

After you've chosen your path, committed to it, and created value, you must share your work. You need to build an audience, and then start engaging with Connectors—the people who have a high degree of influence around whatever you're doing. This should happen organically. Don't look for handouts and don't try to pad your contact list. Instead, connect with people you truly admire. These are people you want to emulate, people you want to invite to dinner and talk to for hours. Notice that this is the last step, not the first. This is because connecting is only useful when:

1. You know who you are
2. You have something of value to offer

It's like any relationship. When you go on a date, how do you know if the other person is someone you'd like to fold into your life? At the most basic level, you look for the characteristics that will mesh well with who you are, balance you out, and help you grow. If you don't already have #1 and #2 figured out, the relationship is likely to fail.

The rest of the book will take you through the Four Cs in sequence. The first step is to *choose.*

STEP 1: CHOOSE
PASSION AND PURPOSE

"I'm trying to free your mind Neo, but I can only show you the door. You're the one who has to walk through."

MORPHEUS, *THE MATRIX*

Work Journal #1: Stuck

Before I cofounded a company, I was stuck in Zombie Land. I was working in New York City and my job was painfully boring. My entire department was uninspired—we were all just going through the motions. In an effort to release some angst, I began chronicling the happenings of each day, using my email account as a journal. I wrote the entries as email drafts to avoid any suspicion. That way, I could easily switch over to my actual inbox if a manager or nosey co-worker walked by.

I had forgotten about my secret journal until I started writing this book. I came across it while sifting through old emails. It was fascinating to see how I felt back then. My raw emotions perfectly demonstrate the agony of Zombie-Land, so I've included them throughout the book. Most of the journal entries are in their original form, or edited only slightly for clarity and grammar. They were written nearly a decade ago, providing an authentic glimpse into the mind of my younger self. Here's the first entry:

Circa 2006, Written at Work

So here I am at work, not working. I've decided that my email will become my new journal. This way, I can give the impression that I may be sending an important message to a coworker, when, in actuality, I am trying desperately to make the minutes feel more like minutes and less like hours. It's sad that after all my hard work and schooling, this is what has followed. I was more stimulated at my restaurant job in high school than I am now.

What's my job, you ask? I'm not sure, but let me try to explain. I work for an internet consulting firm. Big clients like eBay and Citigroup come to us for help improving their websites. It sounds like it could be interesting, right? But let me tell you what really goes on. Hold on, I have to go to a meeting...

...I just got out of the meeting and my manager's manager just resigned. The whole department is clearly going down the tubes.

Anyway, let me explain how this dying department works. Jenny from Company X will call us and say, "Hey, we want to make our website better!" Then we come into the picture and start doing some work for Jenny. We put some online surveys together, collect a bunch of data, and then present it in a nice, colorful powerpoint presentation.

Unfortunately, there is no thought behind our work. Our only goal is to please Jenny so that she can please her boss so that everyone can receive their paychecks, and then go home and buy some cheap food and a movie, and fall asleep on their couch, and finally wake up the next morning to repeat the entire ritual over again.

Instead of providing rich data, we provide bullshit data. We ask questions the way Jenny wants us to ask them, whether or not the question will create an unnatural bias, therefore rendering the data corrupt. We spit out literally the same "Impact Report" to every client, even when clients have completely different goals in conducting their research.

I swear, children in middle school could do this stuff. They're more adept at using software anyway. Why the hell are they in school? We should get them into the office and hurry up this whole "life" thing. Why waste time in school when, inevitably, they will end up sitting in front of a computer, crunching numbers for someone who won't understand or care what those numbers mean? We should get all these middleschoolers to join the party early! Yes, I'm being sarcastic. God, if I only knew what was coming, I would have failed 8th grade as many times as possible.

You Are the Enemy

So many of us hate our jobs, yet we do nothing to change the situation. If you're one of these people, you need to realize that you (and you alone) have the power to break free. Self-doubt and self manufactured fear keep people in ZombieLand, but escaping isn't as hard as it seems. It's mostly in your head. Let's use one of the great philosophical works of our time to demonstrate. Of course I'm referring to Walt Disney's American classic, *Dumbo*.[9]

Dumbo, the dopey elephant with massive ears, thinks he's a loser. He is constantly ridiculed by his peers for his awkward appearance. When tasked with the improbable feat of flying, Dumbo wallows in self-doubt, convincing himself that it's impossible.

Despite his fear, Dumbo still learns to fly, but only with the aid of a magic feather. When he loses grip of the feather in his final circus act, he freaks out. He thinks he can't fly without it. He plummets toward the ground, but somehow comes out of his dip at the last possible moment, narrowly escaping disaster. He flies triumphantly around the circus without the feather, realizing he never needed it in the first place.

The feather wasn't a magic feather after all. It was a psychological trick to distract Dumbo from his self-doubt. He could fly all along. He just needed the courage to defy his own fear. You don't need a magic feather either, so don't go searching for one. You can start flying *right now*—without the feather.

---

9   http://en.wikipedia.org/wiki/Dumbo

Act Today, Not Tomorrow

"Sooner or later you're going to realize, just as I did,
that there's a difference between knowing
the path and walking the path."

MORPHEUS, *THE MATRIX*

The biggest deterrent to freeing yourself from ZombieLand is inaction—not starting. Don't wait. Your life is slipping away from you one day at a time, and you don't get those days back.

Denver Startup Week was launched in 2012. Here's a description of the event, from their website:[10]

> Since 2012, the most creative and well-connected innovators from Colorado and beyond come together for a week of learning, discussion, networking, and more. In 2013, 5,500+ startup community members and over 650 companies engaged in over 125 community-driven events, all with the goal of celebrating everything entrepreneurial in the Mile High City.

Bart Lorang, the CEO of a company called Full Contact, sat on a panel that week that discussed the Startup Colorado Community Fund. The fund was created to assist entrepreneurs with community focused initiatives, to further support Colorado's burgeoning startup ecosystem. During the panel, Bart unintentionally coined the term

---

10   http://www.denverstartupweek.com/

Doerocracy.[11] He used the term to describe the meritocratic and proactive nature of startup communities. Here's Bart's account of what happened:

> Phil asked the panel for advice on how to get plugged in and [get] help. When it got to me, my response was simple: "Our startup community is a Doerocracy. If you get shit done, you can be a leader." I made up the word Doerocracy on the spot, but I think it describes the dynamic well. There is no Vice President of Membership to the Startup Community. It's open to all [who] want to participate. If you want to be a leader, simply *do* stuff. Don't ask anyone else's permission. That's what a Doerocracy is.

I hope the term *Doerocracy* sticks. It's a great way to describe the mindset of a leader. And it doesn't just apply to startups. While startups are emblematic of leadership and innovation, the concept of a Doerocracy transcends all communities and institutions. Any leader, in any environment, will tell you that the key ingredient to making progress is also the most obvious: stop thinking and start doing.

Any Action Is Still Action

Can't take the big leap? It's okay. Start small. But do *something*.

---

11   http://tinyurl.com/pyefh2c

I first contemplated writing a book years before it actually happened. I didn't take the leap because I didn't have enough experience. But that was okay. I started writing blog posts and jotting down ideas for the book whenever anything relevant sparked my interest. I never published the blog posts. I just kept them to myself. I saved my favorite articles so I could refer back to them later. I read books that I thought could help direct my writing style or give me additional inspiration. All of this was done *prior to deciding* to write the book. It was simply interesting to me, so I did it. When it finally came time to write the book, most of the preliminary steps had already been taken, which made it much less daunting to get started, and accelerated the process.

Build up your experience in increments. If you're truly passionate about something, this should happen naturally over time. When you're finally ready to take the big leap, it won't feel like such a big leap anymore. It'll just feel like the next step.

Why It's So Easy to Feel Off Track

Samuel Stouffer was a sociologist who performed a number of behavioral studies within the United States Army during World War II. During the course of his research, Stouffer noticed something peculiar: In departments that offered more frequent and regular promotions, people were less satisfied with their promotion program. Wait—if it was *easier* to get promoted, why were people *less* happy?

As it turns out, being promoted in a promotion-friendly environment doesn't make anyone feel particularly happy or proud, because it's so common. It just makes the people who *aren't* promoted feel horrible. Conversely, in an environment with a more exclusive promotion program, the select few who are promoted feel a sense of accomplishment, while everyone else still feels fine since promotions are so hard to come by. Essentially, in the latter case, the vast majority of people end up in the non-promotion boat, so they don't feel alone. If a promotion isn't expected, we don't think twice about getting one. But if it's expected and we don't get one, we feel like crap. We measure ourselves based on how we perform *relative to our local environment*. In sociology, this is known as "relative deprivation" (RD).

Malcolm Gladwell discusses the concept of RD in *David and Goliath*,[12] a book about underdogs. He goes into great detail about a young girl who attended Brown University. Although she was extremely intelligent on an absolute scale, she felt inadequate when comparing herself to the relatively high concentration of even *smarter* students at her elite college. The phenomenon occurs on a global scale, too. Gladwell explains that the suicide rate in the happiest countries (Switzerland, Denmark, Iceland, the Netherlands, Canada) is actually higher than the suicide rate in countries that are reportedly less happy (Greece, Italy, Portugal, Spain). Why? Because even the smallest amount of unhappiness can make you feel miserable in a happy country. When everyone else around you is smiling, you're more likely to feel like an outcast if you experience *any* depression at all, which then just compounds the issue.

---

12   Malcolm Gladwell, *David and Goliath*. (Little, Brown and Company, 2013).

Relative deprivation is bound to happen as we move through life. Competition in the workplace naturally stiffens as we advance. This is expected, so we can usually deal with that. But what if we were also constantly feeding ourselves a skewed perspective of our local environment that made things seem even *worse*? What if our social and professional circles appeared more competitive and glorified than they actually were? Unfortunately, this is precisely what's happening in the digital age, as a result of something called the "Generalized Friendship Paradox."

Allow me to explain. In 1991, the sociologist Scott Feld discovered that people, on average, have fewer friends than their friends have. Or, looking at it the other way around, your friends have more friends than you.[13] It holds true for other types of relationships, too. For example, your sexual partners are likely to have more sexual partners than you. It makes sense. If someone has lots of friends, you're more likely to be among those friends. If someone has lots of sexual partners, you're more likely to be among those partners. But what about other characteristics like intelligence, wealth, and happiness? Are your friends also likely to be smarter, richer, and happier than you?

Social physicists Young-Ho Eom and Hang-Hyun Jo have already answered this question for us, and the answer is *yes*. They completed a series of studies relating to published scientists, showing that if a scientist writes a scientific paper, his co-authors will have more co-authors, more citations, and more publications than he does. Essentially, his

---

13   http://en.wikipedia.org/wiki/Friendship_paradox

colleagues will be more accomplished.[14] Generally then, this can be applied to other characteristics within a network, including happiness, intelligence, and wealth. This is known as the "Generalized Friendship Paradox" (GFP).

Here's where this gets interesting. Because social networks like Facebook and Twitter are such highly trafficked networks, we now experience the GFP in our daily lives. So, putting this all together: We are likely to have friends who have more friends than us. Those friends are likely to be smarter, wealthier, and happier than us. Those friends are also likely to post about themselves more frequently on social media. This creates a situation where others feel inclined to mimic the behavior. Even friends who are less accomplished or less happy will try to seem equally as happy or accomplished, just to keep pace.

You can see how this creates a problem. If we combine the concept of relative deprivation with the Generalized Friendship Paradox, we get the following recipe for disaster:

1. We tend to measure our competence by those around us (RD).
2. We're constantly observing people within our social networks who appear better than us (GFP).

It's one thing to see celebrities on TV and in magazines, but it's another thing entirely to feel like our immediate friends and colleagues are celebrities, too. It's no wonder that most of us feel inadequate or doubtful about ourselves.

---

14   http://arxiv.org/abs/1401.1458

There are two things to consider here. First, you have to ask yourself whether or not you're satisfied with your life, *without making irrelevant comparisons.* Do you dislike your job because it's not right for you, or because you're comparing yourself to a professional skydiver who keeps posting breathtaking photos in your Facebook feed?[15] Second, and more importantly, if you legitimately aren't satisfied, why aren't you doing anything about it? You have to be careful because the reality is sometimes hard to see. There's a lot of crap in the way to cloud your judgement. Big decisions always come with qualms. But you can feel more confident in your choices if you understand the *true* motivation behind them.

You're not less intelligent, less wealthy, and less happy than everybody else, but unfortunately, the shiny façades of the social arena are likely to make you feel that way. You have to remember that social media is constantly feeding you a false representation of the world—a world that seems increasingly more fantastic and unattainable. You have to look beyond the façades and realize it's mostly BS. The best thing you can do is ignore it. The current happenings in cyberland have nothing to do with your stature in the world, your capabilities, or your happiness. *You* get to decide all of that. Once you've pushed the BS aside, you can more accurately assess your situation.

If you're considering starting a company, quitting your job, starting a side project, ending a relationship, etc., your

---

15   This applies to more than just your job. The same principle applies to your love life, accomplishments, or anything else you might measure by comparing yourself with those in your social networks.

stature or reputation in the outside world *should not* be a factor in your decision. What *should* be the basis of your decision, then? Passion, my friend.

Passion Is the Currency of Happiness

If you feel you don't have a big enough reason to flee ZombieLand, you're not alone. Knowing that social media skews our perspective is one reason to be cautious. And being bored at work isn't a life-threatening situation, right? Not so fast.

According to the always-brilliant Tim Ferriss (author of *The Four Hour Workweek*), the opposite of happiness is not unhappiness—it's boredom, and I'm 100% in agreement. Most of us work because we need to make money, but we're bored while doing it. Since the bulk of our time is spent working, we become unhappy. This isn't a small problem. It's a *colossal* problem.

If we follow Tim's thinking, the key to maintaining happiness is simply avoiding boredom. I've found passion, purpose, entertainment, and excitement to be the best cures. Fortunately, most of these cures can be experienced for free—especially passion.[16] The problem is how most of us fill our time. If it were possible to earn a comfortable living by doing something boring for ten minutes and then filling the rest of our day with passion—that would be a good equation for maintaining happiness. Unfortunately,

---

16   Unless you have a passion for buying really expensive things; if this is your passion, good luck.

most of us experience the opposite. We spend an incredibly small amount of time on our passions because the majority of our time is consumed by boring or stressful work. This is what we need to fix. Here's the high level solution:

I call this the Happiness Pyramid. It will improve your decision-making and keep you out of ZombieLand, which is the most common source of boredom. You may have noticed that happiness is nowhere to be found. This is because you can achieve happiness at the very first level of the pyramid. All you need is passion.

Because money determines so much of what we're able to do in life, skipping over passion (and everything else) in order to earn money is the most common scenario. We try to become successful so we can be happy, instead of making sure we're happy so we can become successful. The approach is backwards. If you're spending the bulk of your time doing something primarily for profit, and there's no passion at the foundation, you need to jump ship. Don't fight for profit or anything else in the pyramid. Instead, fight for *time* and then fill it with passion. Once you have a strong foundation of passion, you can begin focusing on the other levels of the pyramid if you want to augment them further.[17]

Making passion the cornerstone of your life is likely an impossibility at the onset. Most of us can't just quit our jobs and go sailing on the Pacific. So, here's how you start: You need to identify what I call *Purpose Spurts*. Purpose Spurts are the simple activities you love to do on a regular basis. Examples include watching a football game, going for a run, or reading a book. These simple pleasures will keep you afloat in the happiness department.

Yes, this is common sense. It's also where most of us stop. We assume we'll only have time for a few Purpose Spurts a month and that the rest of our schedule will be filled with boring crap. Thus, the disease of chronic unhappiness sets in. If you want to escape this, you need to start looking for what I call *Purpose Arcs*. Purpose Arcs are the broader activities that feed your passions. Examples include exercising or teaching. Note that exercising and teaching are general activities with no beginning or end, while watching a football game is a specific activity with a

---

17   You don't necessarily need to seek knowledge, connections, influence, and profit after focusing on passion. Those things will accumulate naturally. The key point is that you should never *skip over* passion to pursue anything above it at the onset. Passion should always be the first basic step in any developmental pursuit.

finite duration. The finite duration is what distinguishes a spurt from an arc.

Defining an arc can help define related spurts, and vice versa. For example:

Arc	Spurt
Teaching	Give 3 private seminars on topic x
Exercising	Workout each morning for 40 minutes

Spurts naturally contribute to fulfilling an arc. **Your goal should be to find spurts that can generate meaningful income.**

The example of giving private seminars, for instance, could be an income-generating spurt that fulfills the arc of *teaching*. This is how you can build an independently funded lifestyle with passion (i.e. happiness) at the core.

Writing this book was a spurt. I started out with smaller spurts like reading other books about lifestyle design, collecting interesting articles, and writing blog posts. I then rolled those activities into the bigger spurt of writing a book. The book is available for purchase, so it was an income-generating spurt. It also contributes to one of my broader Purpose Arcs—*sharing knowledge*. At the core, this income-generating activity was fueled by passion. It ate up a ton of my time, and I absolutely loved it. That's the takeaway.

Starting a company was also a collection of small spurts. Before the company was formed, I would read startup blogs every morning instead of the news. I kept a running list of business ideas. Many of the ideas turned into long documents with feature descriptions and marketing plans. I was doing this because I enjoyed it. It gave me excitement and hope. Eventually, it turned into an income-generating spurt when I finally started a company, years later. It also contributed to another Purpose Arc—*creating products that entertain.*

A Purpose Spurt doesn't necessarily need to exist outside of what we typically categorize as *work*; it just needs to be founded on passion and purpose. If you love cooking and you're a chef by trade, you're golden. Just be honest with yourself. You need to love your craft. Likewise, spurts don't necessarily need to be work-related. Love taking care of your kids? Great. Use that to fuel your happiness. Or, better yet, figure out a way to turn it (or something similar) into an income-generating spurt.

If you're not sure where your passion lies, ask yourself what you end up doing when you have nothing to do. Where does your mind go? What websites do you visit? Which articles and books do you read? What television shows do you watch? Which activities naturally draw your attention? Your passion is right in front of you: it's how you spend your idle time. People say you shouldn't make your passion your work. Bullshit. If you want to avoid ZombieLand, you *must* make your passion your work.[18]

---

18   Not *all* passions are well suited for income-generation. I'll go into greater detail on this later. You may also choose to preserve certain activities as hobbies to deliberately separate them from work. For example, if becoming a sports broadcaster would ruin your love of sports, you should stay away from broadcasting to preserve the experience of watching as a fan.

Meng To's Passion

Meng To (pronounced like "toe") was born in Cambodia, but his family immigrated to Canada when he was eight years old. They were poor. His mother worked multiple jobs to make ends meet and, as a result, they moved around Montreal and Quebec quite a bit. Being a poor Cambodian child in Canada was rough. Meng was constantly on the move, and he was always the strange-looking new kid. Naturally, he didn't make too many friends. He didn't like school either, finding his coursework boring. There wasn't much to be happy about.

But then something happened. Meng's mother scraped together enough cash to buy him a computer, and he loved it. In the computer world, Meng's appearance didn't matter. He could build cool stuff and share it with hundreds of people with the click of a button—and he was judged only by his work. He was in control. He quickly found that he could game the system, too. By downloading software online, he could access new tools without spending a dime.

"You had no choice," Meng explains. "As a student, you can't afford $1,000 software. The internet is really just a community of people self-teaching themselves about whatever is new. And if you were in that movement, I think you had no choice but to learn everything through the computer, because you couldn't learn it at school. It was way too new to be covered as any sort of topic, which is exactly why I felt so disconnected from school back then."

So, after each boring day of class, Meng would come home, sit in front of his computer, and build fan sites of his idols (like Jet Li). Unknowingly, he was cultivating a valuable skillset. And eventually, he would become a master.

The summer before Meng was supposed to go to college, he decided he needed a job. He recalls, "for whatever reason, I didn't want the job to be something non-serious like working at a coffee shop or at a general store. I wanted the job to be serious—representative of my passions." He knew he wanted to design websites. "I was eighteen and I was already thinking, '*This is exactly what I want to do.*'"

Every Passion Is Applicable

It might seem like all of your passions fall into the hobby category. After all, passions are usually fun and work usually isn't. Having fun doesn't pay the bills—the boring stuff does. Right?

It's natural to look at the world through the lense of corporate America and academia. Those institutions tell us to study business, economics, literature, science, math, and history. All of those disciplines are certainly useful, but they aren't all-encompassing. In reality, the world values talent and knowledge in absolutely *anything*.

We know that becoming proficient in things like software design, music, and sports can be valuable, but let's take a look at an even more unconventional skill: playing video games. Playing video games was once considered a hobby, but not anymore. New businesses are cropping up, like Twitch,[19] which streams live online video of gamers

---

19   http://www.twitch.tv/

playing their favorite games. Tournaments have sprouted up around the globe, bringing together the most competitive and skilled gamers on the planet. These professional gamers are earning serious income, some making hundreds of thousands of dollars a year.[20]

To those of us who play video games as a hobby, this seems ridiculous. But these professional gamers are able to fund their lives by playing video games because *they're extremely good at it*. It's taken me half a lifetime to realize that any talent can generate income. *Value* is the key ingredient.[21] If you can make really amazing art out of jelly beans, people will buy it. It just has to be really amazing.

The Air Force Academy Isn't for Everyone

Tyler Ward grew up in Denver, Colorado. After high school, he joined the United States Air Force Academy Prep School, where he also played football. Unfortunately, the military discipline of the program didn't sit well with Tyler. It didn't feel right, so he dropped out.

Tyler moved back home and enrolled at the University of Northern Colorado to start working towards a journalism degree. Maybe writing was always his calling—but not in journalism—in music. He had played the bass at his local

---

20 http://tinyurl.com/p4lr9yp

21 If you're trying to build a lifestyle business (i.e. generate a full salary) from monetizing a passion, you need a sizable market and a high-quality product. If your market is too small or too saturated, you may not be able to generate enough income. More on this later.

church growing up, and he later taught himself to play the guitar. From that point forward, he had a strong passion for music, but never considered it a viable career path. He found himself writing songs in his spare time while working toward his journalism degree. Eventually, he started recording the songs in his parent's basement, which quickly evolved into video recordings. He posted the videos to YouTube, and gradually built up a cult-like fanbase. His songs were good, his videos were well produced, and he was charismatic. He was on to something.

As of this writing, Tyler's YouTube channel has over 1.7 million subscribers. His videos have been viewed over 400 million times. His songs have appeared as high as number five on Billboard's Top 100 Uncharted List and he was also ranked on Billboard's Social 50 Chart for several weeks. He even performed live on The Ellen DeGeneres Show. He's a signed artist, under his own label, as well as Sony Music Germany, and has toured across all of Europe and the United States.

Perhaps Tyler's biggest accomplishment is his aforementioned production company, Tyler Ward Studios (http://tylerwardstudios.com/). He founded the studio in 2009. His mission is to find up-and-coming artists and help them produce radio-quality songs to launch their careers. Former clients include Jason Derulo, Cody Simpson, and The Plain White T's.

Tyler has become a Connector. He is also the quintessential example of a trailblazer. When Tyler attended the Air Force Academy, he was in ZombieLand. There's nothing wrong with the Air Force Academy. It's actually quite prestigious. But it wasn't right for Tyler. He was meant to be working in the music industry. Quitting the Academy was probably tough. It was likely embarrassing, too. But it was the right thing to do.

Now, looking back, Tyler (and everyone else) can see that it was clearly the correct decision. Tyler started without a direction, allowing Purpose Spurts to present themselves organically. When he found something he enjoyed, he quit everything else and latched on, gaining as much experience as possible. It wasn't always pretty. Dropping out of the Air Force Academy, going back to your local college, and making homemade videos in your parent's basement doesn't sound very glamorous—but the setbacks and risks eventually paid off. Tyler now funds his life by pouring all of his energy into his Purpose Arc of sharing and creating music. By the way, he's just about to turn thirty years old. Not bad.[22]

Your Passion is a Product

"What are you trying to tell me,
that I can dodge bullets?"

"No Neo, I'm trying to tell you that
when you're ready, you won't have to."
THE MATRIX

While not everyone has the necessary skills to become the next YouTube popstar, it's possible to turn *any* passion into

---

22 http://en.wikipedia.org/wiki/Tyler_Ward

an income-generating product, in any industry. There are a few reasons why this is the case:

1. People crave knowledge
2. Knowledge is boundless
3. People are lazy
4. People are forgetful

People Crave Knowledge

As we stumble through life, we're constantly looking for ways to improve. Wouldn't it be great if you could learn how to speak ten languages, cook gourmet meals, perform mind-bending magic tricks, design mobile apps, play four instruments, make a million bucks, win any argument, land any job, and find your perfect soulmate? Of course it would.

Knowledge is Boundless

There is infinite knowledge to gain. The quest to get better at life is neverending. This is an awesome premise, but it's also overwhelming. If there's infinite knowledge to gain, we can't possibly learn everything there is to know. When the reality of the neverending quest for knowledge sets in, we realize we have to pick and choose—we have to find a subset of things to focus on. We also need to find efficiencies so we can learn as much as possible, which brings me to my next point.

People are Lazy

Most of us are lazy. If there's a shortcut, we'll take it. We want simplicity. This is a good thing because it gives craftsmen the opportunity to create value. It means people like you and I (the craftsmen) can spend time learning about a particular topic, synthesize the most relevant information about that topic, package it into an organized format (a book, a blog, a podcast, an app, etc.), and sell it to people who are interested in learning about it. Gary Vaynerchuk did this with wine. Leo Babauta did it with forming habits. Tim Ferriss did it with lifestyle design. If you have useful things to say, people will pay to listen.

People are Forgetful

You might be saying to yourself, *"Wait a minute. This all sounds great, but the thing I would teach people about has already been taught. In fact, I've read several books about it! I can't possibly make money from sharing my knowledge if the knowledge already exists."* I understand your thought process here, but you're wrong. Lucky for you, people are forgetful. It doesn't matter if related products already exist. In fact, it's a good thing because it validates your market. Think about your concern—if you've read other books about the topic, it means people have purchased those books. People will consume content about the same topic over and over again. You are your own proof.

Now that you know the basics of why and how you can turn any passion into a product, there are some important realities to consider. (Keep in mind, these rules relate to *any* product, so if you're on the track of building a more traditional company, they still apply):

1. You have to be knowledgeable (or talented).
2. You have to distribute effectively.

3. Blockbusters are rare.
4. You have to seem fresh.
5. You have to provide value.

You Have to be Knowledgeable, (or Talented)

You can't hope to provide value if you aren't either knowledgeable or talented. You need at least one of the two. People can sense bullshit pretty easily, so you should focus on something you know a lot about, or do well. You might be tempted to attack a big market, but if you're not 100% confident and capable in that area, it won't work. You'll fail when you realize the market is saturated and the competition for attention is steep. It's better to find a niche you truly understand, or a specific product category in which you can excel.

You Have to Distribute Effectively

After creating a product, you have to distribute it. You want to find the distribution channel that gives you the best opportunity to reach your target audience. For Tyler Ward, this meant posting videos to YouTube. He could have published his music exclusively on iTunes, but YouTube is far more viral, and it's also more popular among teens, his target demographic. As another example, if you were selling an application, you'd want to distribute it through the major app platforms: The Apple App Store, Kindle App Store, and Google Play.

Blockbusters are Rare

The financial returns from your project may not be substantial enough for you to quit your day job— at least not right away—but your efforts will still be worthwhile. You should be able to derive happiness from working on something you care about, and take pride in creating quality content. Remember, there are various currencies, and passion is the currency of happiness. That's worth a lot, regardless of the financial gain. The final output is also a reflection of your ability, which can work in your favor down the road.

You Have to Seem Fresh

How will customers perceive your product? What will make it better, more fun, and more enjoyable than similar offerings? If it feels boring or redundant, it has no chance.

You Have to Provide Value

This is the most important point. You could execute on every step above, but if the customer isn't getting value from whatever you're selling, your efforts won't matter. This is also the most intangible element in the equation. How do you know what constitutes value? My best advice is to get feedback. Whenever you create content, share it. Consumer behavior is nearly impossible to predict. The best way to test it is to share your product early and often.

Final Thoughts on Creating Content

Creating a product based on your passion is a fantastic thing to do, not only because it can generate income, but because it will teach you about yourself *and* produce a tangible artifact you can be proud of later. Even if you don't strike gold financially, the project will pay dividends in other ways. Selling a product—a book, a song, a game, a podcast, an app, or anything else that you can sell as a distinct unit—is also beneficial because it's easily consumable and it's finite. This means you can fail at one project and succeed at another, without wasting decades of your life.

Packaging your knowledge into a product is just one example of an income-generating Purpose Spurt. While it's possibly the most versatile option, it's not the only option, and may not necessarily be the best option for *you*. As I mentioned, if you're on the track of building a full-fledged company, everything in this section still applies. You still have to be knowledgeable in your product offering. You still have to distribute effectively. Your chances for blockbuster success are slim, so you have to be in it for the long haul. You still have to seem fresh to beat out the competition. And you still have to provide value, or the consumer won't stick. By the way, you also have to deal with culture, team dynamics, market forces, and cash flow. Not easy. This is why passion *must* be at the foundation. You won't persist if you're not committed from the mental standpoint.

Connect the Dots Later

Your passions might seem trivial or useless, but you shouldn't worry about that. You can't possibly understand how the experiences of your past and present will affect your future, and that's a good thing. It gives you the freedom to follow your passions, regardless of their perceived value in the here and now. Remember the video gamers and their six-figure salaries? Remember the homemade videos that turned Tyler Ward into a YouTube sensation? You'd be surprised how passions, hobbies, and even seemingly insignificant knowledge can serve you in your future.

Here's another story from a stubborn college dropout who later realized the value of not knowing his path:

> I dropped out of Reed College after the first six months, but then stayed around as a drop-in for another eighteen months or so before I really quit. So why did I drop out?
>
> It started before I was born. My biological mother was a young, unwed college graduate student, and she decided to put me up for adoption. She felt very strongly that I should be adopted by college graduates, so everything was all set for me to be adopted at birth by a lawyer and his wife. Except that when I popped out they decided at the last minute that they really wanted a girl. So my parents, who were on a waiting list, got a call in the middle of the night asking: "We have an unexpected baby boy; do you want him?" They said: "Of course." My biological mother later found out that my mother had never graduated from college and that my father had never graduated from high school. She refused to sign the final adoption papers. She only relented a few months later when my parents promised that I would someday go to college.
>
> And seventeen years later I did go to college. But I naively chose a college that was almost as expensive as Stanford, and all of my working-class parents' savings were being spent on my college tuition. After six months, I couldn't see the value in it. I had no idea

what I wanted to do with my life and no idea how college was going to help me figure it out. And here I was spending all of the money my parents had saved their entire life. So I decided to drop out and trust that it would all work out okay. It was pretty scary at the time, but looking back it was one of the best decisions I ever made. The minute I dropped out I could stop taking the required classes that didn't interest me, and begin dropping in on the ones that looked interesting.

It wasn't all romantic. I didn't have a dorm room, so I slept on the floor in friends' rooms, I returned coke bottles for the 5¢ deposits to buy food with, and I would walk the seven miles across town every Sunday night to get one good meal a week at the Hare Krishna temple. I loved it. And much of what I stumbled into by following my curiosity and intuition turned out to be priceless later on. Let me give you one example:

Reed College at that time offered perhaps the best calligraphy instruction in the country. Throughout the campus every poster, every label on every drawer, was beautifully hand calligraphed. Because I had dropped out and didn't have to take the normal classes, I decided to take a calligraphy class to learn how to do this. I learned about serif and san serif typefaces, about varying the amount of space between different letter combinations, about what makes great typography great. It was beautiful, historical, artistically subtle in a way that science can't capture, and I found it fascinating.

None of this had even a hope of any practical application in my life. But ten years later, when we were designing the first Macintosh computer, it all came back to me. And we designed it all into the Mac. It was the first computer with beautiful typography. If I had never dropped in on that single course in college, the Mac would have never had multiple typefaces or proportionally spaced fonts. And since Windows just copied the Mac, it's likely that no personal computer would have them. If I had never dropped out, I would have never dropped in on this calligraphy class, and personal computers might not have the wonderful typography that they do. Of course it was impossible to connect the dots looking forward when I was in college. But it was very, very clear looking backwards ten years later.

Again, you can't connect the dots looking forward; you can only connect them looking backwards. So you have to trust that the dots will somehow connect in your future. You have to trust in something—your gut, destiny, life, karma, whatever. This approach has never let me down, and it has made all the difference in my life.

The narrator of this story is Steve Jobs, the legendary CEO of Apple. The story was part of his famous Stanford commencement speech in 2005.[23] It's a perfect illustration of how passion and purpose drive success, not the crossing of an imaginary finish line in the future. Forget the finish

---

23   http://tinyurl.com/dfbkvo

line. It doesn't exist. Instead, look for passion and purpose directly in front of you. The dots will connect later, I promise—and so does Steve.

Work Journal #2: Marcus

People define success in dramatically different ways. When I was stuck in ZombieLand, I was following social convention. People looked at my life and thought I was successful, but I wasn't happy. I was crumbling inside. The 9-5 desk job is the structure fed to us, but that doesn't mean it's the only choice we have. Just take it from my friend Marcus.

Circa 2006, Written at Work

You know those people in college who never graduate? You know who I'm talking about. Everyone has that friend in college who looks like he could be someone's father. This guy lives for the college life. He's unusually calm, has questionable hygiene, and loves life. Everyone looks at this guy and shakes their heads. "Poor fellow," they say. "He needs to get his life together." I think I said that very same thing to our resident super senior, Marcus. I was embarrassed for him then. But now, looking back, I'm envious.

Marcus might be the smartest man alive. He has avoided capitalistic captivity. He has defied the mundane society known as corporate America. Not only that—he's found a way to defy it in style.

Marcus weighs about 250 pounds. He's pure muscle. He gets to use the university fitness center at will because he kept his school ID all these years. The students at the front desk don't seem to bother him too much. Their scanning systems don't register that his ID card has expired, or that he hasn't been a full-time student for over eight years. Regardless, none of the scrawny students working the front desk are going to tell him to leave. The girls swoon as he walks through the turnstiles, and the guys just keep their heads down to avoid pissing him off.

Marcus exercises at the fitness center every day— for free. I've been to every damn gym in the entire city of New York and I can't workout for less than $75 a month.

Marcus lives in my old fraternity house. He's got a place in the basement all to himself. Every day, he comes upstairs at some point and grabs some food. There's a house cook who makes all the meals, so he doesn't have to do anything but eat. Sometimes, it's spaghetti and meatballs, sometimes it's meatloaf, sometimes it's turkey and mashed potatoes. The food isn't spectacular, but it does the trick.

I've been keeping track of my food spending and it works out to about $300 a month lately. Keep in mind, I'm a conservative eater, and I try to budget myself when it comes to food. So, my annual food expense is $3,600. Marcus' expense? Zero.

What does Marcus buy with all of this saved money? Who knows. Most likely beer. Maybe some workout shorts for the gym.

Marcus does a lot of other things with his free time, since his entire day is filled with it. He goes to the bar, he reads, he writes, he relaxes. In my free time, I sleep.

As far as I know, Marcus doesn't have a job. How does he pay for things like rent? Simple. He doesn't. Since the treasurers in the fraternity have been sloppy and unorganized for the past few years, they don't charge Marcus any late fees when he fails to pay the rent. Every year, a new treasurer is elected and, more often than not, the remaining balances of tenants seem to get lost in the transition. The fraternity's debt is usually reconciled by some donation from the national headquarters, or from some fundraising event that will help the fraternity "raise money for good causes throughout the community and the country." Instead of going to the community, the funds get funneled back into the house to pay for the accrued debt of people like Marcus.

Every once in a while, Marcus will do odd jobs. He'll collect used textbooks and sell them back to the campus bookstores. He'll build lofts for incoming freshmen and charge the innocent newcomers an arm and a leg. He'll make t-shirts for the sorority girls and the frat stars, making a handsome profit. At the end of the year, his bank account is fully loaded. He has such low overhead that his income just sits in his account.

With all his free time, Marcus decides to attend some classes on finance to find out what he should do with his money. He learns as much as possible about how to make a little into a lot. In a year, he's earning an extra 10-30% through investing. If he keeps this up, he'll be a millionaire by the time he's thirty-five.

Marcus is a real person. I saw him at a wedding not too long ago. My journal entry is mostly accurate. Marcus didn't stay in college forever though. He became a personal trainer. His gym recently offered him a management position, but he declined. He doesn't want to deal with the politics. Teaching people is his true passion. He's living the life he wants, and he's happy—just as calm as ever.

Marcus is a Connector. If you want to get into personal training, he's the guy you want to know. He's been training for nearly twenty-five years now, and he's very successful at it. Marcus hasn't taken a traditional career path, and his early adult years weren't always completely stable or comfortable. But he's been very creative in figuring out alternative lifestyles that give him freedom. Even now, Marcus gets to make his own schedule, work with the clients he chooses, and spend his days doing what he loves. In college, people thought Marcus was being lazy, but he wasn't. He was enjoying life, exploring his passion, and honing his craft. Let the naysayers shake their heads. Marcus is smiling.[24]

---

24 Noticing a pattern yet? The lifestyle isn't always glamorous, but it almost always culminates in happiness, plus a level of autonomy that's typically impossible in the traditional 9-5 scenario. By the way, Marcus eventually paid off every cent of the debt he owed to his fraternity.

Look for an Aura

The University of Michigan football stadium is known as the Big House. It's one of the largest and most famous stadiums in the country. When Michigan plays a home game, over 100,000 avid fans fill the stands. It doesn't matter who we're playing. I say *we* because Michigan is my alma mater. I'm a diehard fan. Along with millions of others across the globe, I revel in the aura of Michigan's football program.

"Game day" in Ann Arbor, Michigan, is a magical experience. Hours before kickoff, people begin socializing and preparing for the upcoming game. The stadium is nearly a mile south of the university's main campus, so tens of thousands of students and out-of-town visitors make the trek to the Big House on foot. The streets become sidewalks, filled with crowds of fans adorned in maize and blue.[25] Young children, college students, parents, and grandparents, all march to the stadium with a single focus. There are raucous chants, footballs and frisbees, and lots of beer guzzling. The energy in the air is palpable. All of this activity generates an aura, a concentration of energy that can only be produced by a large mass of people who all believe in the same thing.

I love Michigan football. I'm deeply dedicated to it. I haven't missed a game since I first set foot on campus nearly fifteen years ago.[26] The history and tradition of the program dates back to 1879 when Michigan played its first

---

25 These are Michigan's team colors.

26 This includes watching the games on television. I rarely see the games live anymore because I no longer live in Michigan. (Watching every game in person would be borderline insane/awesome, however.)

intercollegiate game. It's a tradition that has touched millions of people. The aura of Michigan football isn't going away. If I stopped caring, the aura would live on—but I won't stop caring. Why? Because being part of something bigger than yourself is magical.

If I could redo college and choose any school, I'd choose Michigan again. Yes, the education was great. Yes, I made amazing friends. But the biggest reason for choosing Michigan again would be the aura of its collegiate football program.

Auras naturally form around things like sports, religions, and political parties. But anything can have an aura. You should be looking for auras in every relationship you cultivate, every project you engage in, and every company you work for (or build). Different auras work for different people. You have to find one that works for you.

While having an aura is a good thing, not having one is equally as bad. There are droves of companies with no aura. If you're in one of these organizations, get out. I worked in a company with no aura for far too long. My department was the result of an acquisition that happened before I was hired, and the upper management never really knew what to do with our team. After two years of punching in and punching out, I quit. That's when I started a company of my own, and I'm glad I took the risk. I found out recently that my department at the old company folded and, frankly, I'm not surprised. I don't know exactly what happened, but I'm sure it had something to do with the aura, or lack thereof.

When you're part of an aura, you're experiencing the essence of being alive. *Caring. Believing. Feeling.* Without it, you're just showing up.

STEP 2: COMMIT
RISK AND PERSISTENCE

"Success is not final, failure is not fatal:
it is the courage to continue that counts."

WINSTON CHURCHILL

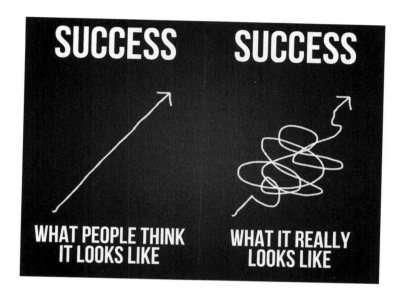

To excel in anything, you must commit. This means sacrifice, focus, and persistence. Commitment also comes with obstacles, failure, and difficult choices.

Many people (myself included) get lost in identifying where our commitment lies. Should you remain at your unfulfilling job in hopes that it will eventually improve? Should you work through a rough patch in your relationship? After thirty years, I've developed a concrete answer that always works, regardless of the situation. You should always commit to:

1. Your feeling of passion
2. Taking risks that bring meaning to your passions

Note that your passions will likely change over time. This means you'll need to make changes throughout your life accordingly. I'm not telling you to dump your partner and quit your job at the first sign of difficulty. I'm telling you to look inwardly at what you truly need—to think critically about what's necessary for you to be consistently happy. (Remember the beach, the mountains, and the swamp?)

Sometimes change will be thrust upon you. If your current business venture fails, life goes on. That type of failure will certainly sting, but if your passion remains, there are always new channels from which to explore it. Never forget that.

Also note that taking risks is a constant and recurring part of the process. Being comfortable with your lifestyle is great, but if you're truly committed to making your passions meaningful, you'll always look for new ways to push the envelope and keep things fresh. This section focuses on many of the issues you'll encounter as you strive to commit to your passions. It will also shed light on the most common excuses for giving up or not starting, and show you how to stay the course. This is arguably the most difficult step of the Four Cs to master.

Prepare to Fail

If you plan on following your passions and pushing your limits, failure is par for the course. Here's an amazing secret that most people are too scared to discover: Connectors don't care if you fail. They know that failure is a dot on a line. If you've stayed true to yourself and nurtured your relationships, your supporters will continue to support you for being brave, as any true friend would. This is where your relationships are measured. This is also where breakthroughs happen. Take it from fitness expert, Tony Horton:

> Failure and success are siamese twins; they don't exist without each other. There's no way around it. The problem with the word "failure" is that it connotes that you're a loser—and losers don't succeed or get the girl (or guy or pie or pot of gold or whatever it is you wanna get). As a result, many people would rather play it safe, not take chances, not explore, and never, ever stick their neck out and actually *try*.
>
> Most people don't realize that failure is the key to joy, happiness, and growth. If you're afraid to fail, then you'll never expose yourself to opportunities for success. On the other hand, if you view failure as awesome, then you'll be open to trying things—and falling on your face, screwing up, making mistakes, and blowing it once in a while. Sucking at something every once in a while is how you achieve greatness in the long run.[27]

You Get Out What You Put In...Sort Of

Risking failure to achieve success seems like a fair trade, but it would be nice to have some insurance—a guarantee of

---

27 Tony Horton, *The Big Picture: 11 Laws That Will Change Your Life.* (Harper Wave, 2014).

being rewarded, at least in part, for our efforts. Has any-one ever told you, "You get out what you put in"? I've heard it a hundred times. It makes logical sense—work hard and you'll get better results than if you slack off.

Let's use basketball as an example. Lebron James is one of the best basketball players to ever play the game. He's shattered numerous records, earned multiple MVP awards, and won multiple national championships. Do you think Lebron would be as successful if he never went to the gym, never practiced, and never listened to his coaches? Proba-bly not. And do you think he'd get paid as much if he wasn't as good? Would he have as many fans? Would he demand as much respect? Probably not. Lebron has natural talent, but he also works extremely hard to achieve greatness.

What if, in some strange alternate universe, Lebron James decided to become a horse jockey instead of a basket-ball player? If he worked just as hard, would he get the same results? Let's look at what it takes to be a horse jockey. Here's some information from my trusty sidekick, Wikipedia:

> Jockeys must be light to ride at the weights which are assigned to their mounts. There are horse carrying weight limits, that are set by racing authorities. The Kentucky Derby, for example, has a weight limit of 126 lb (57 kg) including the jockey's equipment. The weight of a jockey usually ranges from 108 to 118 lb (49 to 54 kg). Despite their light weight, they must be able to control a horse that is moving at 40 mph (64 km/h) and weighs 1,200 lb (540 kg). Though there is no height limit for jockeys, they are usually

fairly short due to the weight limits. Jockeys typically stand around 4 ft 10 in (1.47 m) to 5 ft 6 in (1.68 m).

Lebron James is six foot eight, and weighs over 250 pounds—not exactly the ideal body type for a horse jockey. He could starve himself, run twenty miles a day, and try to lose 150 pounds, but it would be *extremely* difficult given his height. He'd be as thin as a rail. He could practice racing horses, but his height would make it awkward and difficult to master the standard jockey riding form. Even if Lebron dedicated his life to becoming a great horse jockey, he'd likely never become the best jockey of all time. And even if he somehow did, the benefits of being a star horse jockey would be significantly less glamorous than being a star basketball player. Basketball is a far more popular sport, with more opportunity for fame and fortune.

Here's the point: You get out what you put in—*to a degree.* Your natural ability and strengths play a big role in determining the potential of your output. Don't work on things that don't play to your strengths and passions. Don't work on things that provide opportunities that don't interest you. It's easy to get lost in the fight, and continuously bang your head against the wall when people tell you that you get out what you put in. That expression tells us to just keep working harder, regardless of the task. This isn't always the answer. If you're working hard and don't feel like you're getting out what you're putting in, you probably need to stop banging your head against the wall and jump ship.

There is also a time factor here, which is very important to consider. YouTube was acquired by Google for $1.65

billion in 2006, less than two years after its founding.[28] Pop-
Cap, a gaming company, was acquired by Electronic Arts
for $750 million in 2011, eleven years after its founding.[29] If
you founded or worked for either of these companies and
loved every moment of it, the difference in time-to-acqui-
sition is a non-factor. But, if you did *not* enjoy yourself and
didn't grow along the way, you better hope you were working at YouTube. Two years of stagnant personal growth is
far less painful than eleven.

The example above includes two companies that both
sold for a bunch of money, which is great. But there's more
to life than money. There's an *opportunity cost* to everything you do. If you're hitting a wall for more than a year
and you're unhappy, I recommend jumping ship—even if
there's a potential pile of cash down the road. There are opportunities beyond whatever you're currently working on.
Forget how much time, effort, and money has already been
invested and ignore whatever you might be giving up if you
leave. Those are sunk costs and unknown outcomes. Instead, think about what you're working on and who you're
working with *right now*. Then decide if that's really how you
want to be spending your days. That's all that really matters.

I worked at my startup for seven years. I got a lot out
of it, but probably not as much as I put in. Why? Because I
couldn't muster up the work ethic to fully commit and produce real value. Because I was working on something that I
wasn't entirely passionate about or particularly good at. Because I wasted my energy being stressed instead of learning

---

28   http://en.wikipedia.org/wiki/YouTube
29   http://en.wikipedia.org/wiki/PopCap_Games

new skills. I was putting a lot of time in, but it was unproductive time. It's easy to trick ourselves into thinking we deserve a reward because we put the time in, but it doesn't work that way. The commitment has to produce results. The effort has to *matter*.

Keep Adding Dots

When I left my company, I had two options. I could be bitter and angry, or I could accept failure. After some initial rage, I chose the latter. As I transitioned out of the company, I pondered my next move. I had wanted to write a book for years, but it seemed like an unrealistic goal. When you don't have a job, you get a lot of unintentional pressure to find a new one. It's not anyone's fault, it's just the script our society is trained to follow. People wanted to know where I was headed next, and I didn't have an answer for them. "Have you sent your resume out?", they would ask. It stung every time I heard it because I didn't want to "send my resume out". To me, that meant going back to ZombieLand, which sounded horrible.

In the last few months leading up to my departure, I devised a plan called *Screw It, I'm Doing it Anyway*. I decided to write the book. The main impetus for the decision came from a voice buried deep in my soul. It was the voice of my previously confident self, the voice that always told me to do crazy things.

If you ever get a chance to spend time with someone extraordinary, ask them about their hardest times. They'll have plenty of stories for you. They'll tell you about the time that everything nearly fell apart, the moment when things couldn't possibly work out. Failure. Doubt. More failure. Then success. These people usually tell you their stories at the end of that sequence, but all of the steps are still there.

The voice in my soul wouldn't shut up because it had found a reason for the book to be written: To let people know that success and failure are both dots on a line. We experience our lives between the dots. The wisest people are those who constantly work toward the next dot, bringing excitement to the time in between. They relish the opportunity to reflect on their endeavors, in both success *and* failure. Each dot generates powerful lessons, valuable memories, and compelling stories. So there's really only one question to ask yourself: Are you adding dots to your line?

Learn to Love Experiments

Failure can feel like the ultimate death sentence, but it's actually a step forward. When we fail, life is pushing us in a different direction so we can experience something new. One adventure has ended and another is about to begin, because it *must*.

Think of your activities in life as scientific experiments. Scientists expect the vast majority of their tests to fail, but they still view each test as a step forward, regardless of the outcome. This is because each failed test rules out that particular approach, narrowing the remaining scope of potential solutions. You might be thinking, *"What if all of my experiments fail until the day I die?"* Great question. That might happen, depending on how you define failure and success. Here's the magical solution to that problem: The results of your experiments are of little consequence. Only the experiments themselves matter.

The old platitude is true: *It's about the journey, not the destination.* Doing experiments will account for 99% of your time on this earth. That's the journey. The result of your experiments is the other 1%. If you enjoy 99% of your life (the time spent in experimentation), who cares about the results? This is how to remove the problem of failure. Failure is just a temporary result. Its effect is as big or as small as you allow it to be.

Elon Musk is becoming a household name. He cofounded Paypal. He now runs two companies simultaneously. The first, Tesla Motors, builds electric cars. The second, SpaceX, builds rocket ships. Many people think of Elon Musk as a real-world Iron Man—a superhero. He's a living legend. He works extremely hard, and he's brilliant.

Did you know that Elon Musk never worked at Netscape? This is interesting because he actually wanted to work there very badly. He applied to Netscape while he was in grad school at Stanford, but never received a response. He even went to Netscape's lobby with resume in hand, hoping to talk to someone about getting a job. No one in the lobby ever spoke to Elon that day. After getting nervous and feeling ashamed of himself, he walked out.

That's right. Elon Musk failed to get hired at Netscape. The recruiting managers didn't see a need for him, and he was too ashamed to keep badgering them. So what happened next? Well, we know what happened from there.

Musk went on to become one of the most successful and respected visionaries of our time.[30]

Take a deep breath and realize that there are no life-ending failures, only experiments and results. It's also important to realize that *you* are not the failure—the experiment is the failure. It is impossible for a person to be a failure. A person's life is just a collection of experiments. We're meant to enjoy them and grow from them. If you learn to love the process of experimentation, the prospect of failure isn't so scary anymore.

Success Feels Better Than Failure

I don't know for sure, but Elon Musk probably felt horribly embarrassed, and defeated, as he walked out of Netscape's lobby. That's because he didn't want to fail—he didn't expect it. Taking risks is sometimes uncomfortable, and it *should* be.

There's a prevalent philosophy within the startup ecosystem, and it's spreading to the mainstream: *Failure is okay*. This philosophy exists because building startups is insanely hard. Most of them fail. Many entrepreneurs lose sleep, friendships, and even their lives, over the fact that they failed. Giving young companies permission to screw-up is important, not just because it encourages the founders to take bigger risks, but because it helps them maintain their sanity if things fall apart.

---

30   http://youtu.be/L-s_3b5fRd8?t=3m9s

Unfortunately, this philosophy is also very dangerous. It gives the wannabes an invitation to pretend. It gives the slackers an easy excuse. ("If a project fails, oh well! There is nothing and no one to blame, because failure is imminent.") If you follow the wannabe mentality, that's all you will ever be. You'll ultimately end up unhappy, and you'll piss everyone else off in the process. Even though failure is par for the course, it's never the goal.

Not surprisingly, success feels way better than failure. It also breeds more opportunity. If an investor is pitched by two companies with similar products and similar teams, and Team A is lead by a founder with two successful exits while Team B is lead by a founder with two failures, the investor will choose Team A without hesitation. Past performance isn't always indicative of future success, so it's admittedly possible for Team B to prevail—but in the scenario above, you want to be on Team A.

Commit to taking risks that feed your passion. Get used to being nervous and uncomfortable. If you fail, you fail. Accept it, learn from it, and move on. But never *expect* failure. Expect success.

Meng To's Commitment

Remember Meng To, the Cambodian boy living as an immigrant in Canada? Well, there's more to his story. He found a job opening with a design firm the summer before his freshman year, which was great news—except that they wanted him to work full-time, indefinitely. It was either college, or the job. Meng decided to take a risk, and he fully expected to parlay it into a success. He didn't go to college. Instead, he took a job that would help him hone his craft. It wasn't a hard decision at the time. Meng recalls, "I just thought, *I'm going to have a job, it's going to be really well paid, and I'm going to do shit that I love doing.* And that was it."

Here's some advice from Meng: "If you don't care about school, don't do it. But if you do care about school, that's fine—go for it. As long as you are hardworking, you will find success somewhere along the path." That last part is worth repeating: *As long as you are hardworking, you will find success somewhere along the path.* Hard work and dedication have always been a part of Meng's life—so much so that they became ingrained in his character.

He explains: "It's important to be surrounded by non-lazy people. It's important to have an environment where people inspire you to work harder, and I think I was fortunate enough to live in that environment. My mom is one of the hardest working people I've ever had in my life. Today, she's fifty-four and she still works seventy hours a week. It's just insane. When you're surrounded by that kind of person, you have no choice but to say, *If I don't do anything [with myself], I'm going to feel like I'm missing out, or I'm going to feel really frustrated with myself.* It's a lot of discipline."

Meng worked at the design firm for a short time, but he knew he wanted more. "As soon as I left that first job, I knew that I wanted to start my own company." He got started by building an online community for artists, but it made very little money. He did freelance work on the side to pay the bills. "I eventually had to close the company. We didn't make enough."

After closing up shop, Meng tried again. He built a social network, but unfortunately, there was another social network on the rise at the same time. "Facebook got really huge, as you know, so we had to close down that community [too]." It was deflating, going from failure to failure. "I went into that dark time where I had to question what I needed to do in order to be successful."

Meng eventually realized that learning to code could help him succeed. In those days, designers were usually just artists, and programmers were usually just coders. There wasn't much overlap between the two disciplines. By combining them, Meng could develop a unique set of skills, and be almost entirely self-sufficient in bringing new ideas to market.

For a time, Meng worked primarily as a programmer. It wasn't his direct passion, but he was building his skillset. There was even a stretch where he had to move back home with his mother and work at a call center because it was the only work he could find at the time. But all the while, Meng kept learning, kept improving his design portfolio, kept coding, kept *working hard*. Through all of the pit-stops, detours, and setbacks, his commitment to passion and risk always guided his actions. He knew that his failures were just part of the process—just dots on the line.

Work Journal #3: Commit to the Roses

Circa 2006, Written at Work

Time has a way of messing with you. When you want it to speed up, it slows down. Then, when you look back, everything has passed you by, and you never got a chance to stop and smell the roses. There aren't any roses in my office, but if there were, I'd get a good, long whiff. Right now, time is standing still.

I have a stress ball in my hand. It's not really relieving any stress, but it's passing the time a little. It's 3:03 p.m. on a Monday. It can't get much worse than this. The florescent lights in our office appear dimmed. My computer screen is starting to get that hazy glow around it. In reality, my eyes are just going in and out of focus because I've been staring blankly at this damn monitor for so long.

The beige walls of the office are blending into the beige carpeting, which is blending in with my beige desk. Here I am in the middle of New York City—I've made it all the way here, and all I can see is beige. Not the Empire State Building, not the Chrysler Building, not Central Park or Times Square—just beige. In a few hours, I'll leave the office, head down the bumpy elevator, out the door, and into the cold city. It will already be dark. I'll walk a block and then disappear into the subway, leaving the city behind.

Do you ever feel like time is standing still? If so, there's a good chance you're in ZombieLand. Ask yourself how you want to be spending your time. Do you want to be watching the clock and staring at beige walls all day? Or do you want to be swept up in the moment, and lose track of time altogether? Stopping to smell the roses sucks when there are no roses to smell. Commit to the roses. Commit to purpose, and time will take care of itself.

Life Is a Golf Course

What if your desire to take a risk, make a change, or push your limits, is actually just an attitude problem—an issue of perception? What if you're doing the best you can do, and any deviation from your current routine will only cause things to get worse? It's quite possible that you could hit the eject button on ZombieLand, embark on a new project, and fall flat on your face. If you jump ship and then fail at your next endeavor, you've taken a step backwards. Is it really worth the risk? The answer is yes, *absolutely*.

The supposition that the grass is never greener on the other side is bullshit—it's a fallacy. Perception is reality. If you're dissatisfied, why would you stay put? Do you really think there is no scenario in which you would ever feel truly happy, or at least more fulfilled than you feel now? Do you really think the world is *that* unforgiving? Don't fall prey to the *grass is greener* fallacy. It's only useful for one thing—settling.

If you were in an ice cream parlor and samples were free, would you forego the samples and just pick the flavor that sounded the best? No. You'd sample your top choice to make sure it was amazing—and if it wasn't completely mind-blowing, you would try at *least* a few other flavors just to be sure you were making the best choice. This is the process for choosing *ice cream*. Yet, when choosing our path in *life*, we often just accept our current situation and assume there's no better option, despite the constant nagging feeling that we're fooling ourselves. Bigger life decisions might come at a greater cost than an ice cream sample, but the positive effects can be equally impactful.

Sometimes the grass is not greener on the other side. But sometimes it is. If you're not fulfilled, there's a good chance that greener pastures lay elsewhere. Assuming the grass is never greener on the other side is an assumption based on fear and self-doubt. The undeniable truth is that every patch of grass is different. Life is a massive golf course. There's a patch of grass, somewhere, that is mind-blowingly good for you. You have to find that patch.

Hopping Jobs

Common belief: Working at a single company for a long period of time builds credibility, while hopping jobs builds suspicion. This is wrong. More importantly, it misses the point.

Sometimes, to stay committed to your passions, you must decommit from a particular job. Powerful people are looking for risk-takers, not paper pushers. They will value the body of knowledge you've acquired, not the average length of time you've spent at each position. Working at a startup as an intern, then working for a non-profit, then traveling the world, then freelancing, then joining another company—that's an interesting story. That story involves learning, courage, and leadership. In most cases, that type of story will carry the same (if not more) weight than working at a single company for ten years and climbing your way up the corporate ladder.

Be careful though—the idea is not to hop jobs for the sake of hopping. The idea is to do valuable and impressive things with your time. Don't sit idle if you aren't growing. Likewise, if you're working on something valuable and you're passionate about it, don't ditch it for something new at the first sign of difficulty. The value of your work, and your passion for it, are the elements that should drive your decision to hop—or not.

Jump Ship

If you've lost passion for what you're working on, confront it immediately. Ask yourself whether it's a permanent or temporary dip. If you're falling back into ZombieLand (feeling consistently bored and insignificant), it might be time to jump ship. It's critical that you base your decision on passion, and nothing else. I'm reiterating this because there are plenty of bad reasons to quit that are not obviously bad. Here are a few:

- The going gets tough
- Something unexpected slows you down
- People say you won't succeed

- You have too many other things going on
- Stiff competition emerges
- You have a new, better idea

These might seem like legitimate reasons to quit, but they're not. They're just obstacles and distractions.

Everyone who challenges the status quo is faced with obstacles to overcome. Seth Godin calls these inevitable obstacles *The Dip*. In his brilliant little book of the same name, he describes the intricacies of knowing when to quit and when to stick—and why it's so important to learn how to do this effectively. Seth gives a pertinent example of the entrepreneur-wannabe:

> Do you know an entrepreneur-wannabe who is on his sixth or twelfth new project? He jumps from one to another, and every time he hits an obstacle, he switches to a new, easier, better opportunity. And while he's a seeker, he's never going to get anywhere.
>
> He never gets anywhere because he's always switching lines, never able to really run for it. While starting up is thrilling, it's not until you get through the Dip that your efforts pay off. Countless entrepreneurs have perfected the starting part, but give up long before they finish paying their dues. The sad news is that when you start over, you get very little credit for how long you stood in line with your last great venture.[31]

---

31   Seth Godin, *The Dip: A Little Book That Teaches You When To Quit (And When to Stick)*. (Portfolio Hardcover, 2007).

Quitting isn't always bad, but it needs to be done for the right reasons, and never for the wrong ones. It's never black and white, but it always comes back to passion. Read *The Dip*. It will help.

Get a New Car

"Quitting doesn't always mean 'giving up.' Sometimes it means having the integrity to admit that a plan you've invested time and energy into isn't working. Having the strength to walk away means that you can begin to invest anew in something you do love. It's worth the risk."

TONY HORTON

Stewart Butterfield is a well known name in the tech community. Butterfield cofounded Flickr, which was sold to Yahoo in 2005 for a reported $35 million.[32] In 2009, he started another company called Tiny Speck. The company's vision was to create an immersive and constantly evolving virtual world game, accessible from any browser. He called it Glitch.

The team spent several years working on Glitch, but it never caught on with a mainstream audience. The game was shut down in 2012 due to a lack of traction. Butterfield and his team had spent nearly four years working on a failed project. It was a painful setback—but it wasn't "game over."

---

32 http://tinyurl.com/lr5wnyl

While working on Glitch, the team had built an internal productivity tool to streamline communication, and it was very effective. Instead of shutting down Tiny Speck, Butterfield decided to refocus the company around the productivity tool. They would polish and retool their internal app for external distribution, selling it to other companies with a SAAS (Software as a Service) pricing model. They called the new product Slack. The early traction for Slack was outstanding. In 2014, the company (now also known as Slack) raised $42.8 million in a new round of funding from several top tier venture firms. Later that year, they raised another $120 million, valuing the company at over $1 billion.[33]

Your project might fail. But if your project fails, you don't necessarily need to abandon your underlying passion. It's like driving. When your car stops running, you don't give up on the prospect of ever driving again—you get a new car so you can get back on the road. Butterfield knew he had a passion for startups, and he knew that startups were tough. When his vehicle broke down, he didn't stop driving. He took his broken car to the dump, got a new one (with far more horsepower), and slammed his foot back down on the gas pedal.

Don't Get a New Cage

When things go well, you may have the urge to expand—take funding, hire employees, buy an office. These things

---

33   http://www.crunchbase.com/organization/tiny-speck

are exciting, but they can also be suffocating. If you build an organization with yourself at the core, you may end up with less freedom than you had in ZombieLand. You'll be responsible for others, and *answering to others* in many cases. As you build out whatever you're working on, be extremely wary of this. Bigger isn't always better. Here's a poignant analogy from *Rework,* written by the founders of 37Signals:

> Do we look at Harvard or Oxford and say, "If they'd only expand and branch out and hire thousands more professors and go global and open other campuses all over the world ...then they'd be great schools." Of course not. That's not how we measure the value of these institutions. So why is it the way we measure businesses?[34]

What are you chasing after? More praise? More money? More power? More importantly, what is it that you need to *defend* in order to be happy? Your time? Your ability to think creatively? The freedom to make decisions? It might be one of these, all three of these, or none of these. Whatever it is, you better find out. Otherwise, it's quite possible to escape ZombieLand only to lock yourself in a new cage that's even *more* confining. When a commitment to passion serves as the crux of your decision-making process, it's easier to avoid this pitfall.

---

34 Jason Fried and David Heinemeier Hansson, *Rework.* (Crown Business, 2010).

Be Selfish

What if you've lost passion for something that involves other people? Should you forego quitting in the interest of honoring your commitment to the group?

No. You still need to quit. Unfortunately, without passion, you can no longer deliver on your commitment. By honoring a commitment you no longer support, you are lying to yourself and to the other party. When you lose passion, you become the weakest link in the chain, and that holds *everyone* back. While the other party might urge you to stay, it's actually in both of your best interests to remove yourself from the situation.

Adam Smith was an economist from the eighteenth century. He is seen by many as the father of modern economics. He used a metaphor called *the invisible hand* to describe the self-regulating nature of free markets. He theorized that acting out of self-interest creates the optimal outcome for society as a whole.[35] While he spoke of the invisible hand in the context of free markets, it can be applied to other social situations, too—like quitting. As it turns out, acting out of self-interest to better your situation usually benefits everyone. Applying this unnatural truth to your life is an extremely powerful aid in making difficult decisions.

---

35   http://en.wikipedia.org/wiki/Invisible_hand

Meng To's Struggle

When Meng To was building companies and freelancing, he found himself hopping from failure to failure. He went through some dark times as he struggled to find his purpose. But then, in 2007, the iPhone came along. Suddenly, design was not only important, it was the focus. Meng was reinvigorated to find his dream job, and he knew where to look.

"My dream was always to work in the US," he says matter-of-factly. "It's kind of the same as an actor wanting to go to Hollywood. San Francisco (and Silicon Valley) was *the* place. If you were serious about design or serious about engineering, that was the place to be. So I decided that I would do everything I could to get a job there."

And Meng did get a job there. He worked in Silicon Valley for about eighteen months, at which point another curve ball came flying at his head. His visa expired. He knew it was coming, but getting a new one turned out to be far more difficult than he expected. His employer decided to drop him from payroll, and no one else would hire him because of the visa situation. Meanwhile, there were expensive rent and healthcare issues looming. Ultimately, he failed to acquire a new visa in time, so he had to leave.

Meng was yet again forced to do something new with his life. Failure kept knocking him down. What next? Did he go back to Canada and get a 9-5? Nope. He instead decided to travel for a year with his longtime girlfriend. In the meantime, he began working on personal projects again, eventually latching on to a new software called Sketch.

Sketch is a web and mobile design software program built specifically for designers. With Meng's growing knowledge of Sketch and his previous knowledge of design and programming, he was in a unique position. He had acquired a vast array of skills that most designers and programmers lacked. There had been plenty of setbacks throughout his journey, but Meng could finally see the puzzle pieces fitting together. He knew exactly what to do next. All of his hard work and dedication was about to pay off.

Hard Work, Dedication

To do truly meaningful work, you need to get serious, focus, and go all in. Floyd Mayweather Junior is the best pound-for-pound boxer in the world. As of this writing, he is also the highest paid athlete in the world. His motto? *Hard Work, Dedication.* His team chants the motto as he trains. One group yells, "Hard work!" and the other responds, "Dedication!" The chants get louder and faster as Mayweather increases the speed and intensity of his workout.

Mayweather knows the value of these words, and the impact they have on success. He lives by them. He endures grueling training sessions, 2-3 times per day. He often trains late into the night. He doesn't smoke or drink alcohol—ever. Floyd Mayweather is no joke. He's the real deal. And that's why he's such a *big* deal. He lives to box. It's what he loves to do. His hard work and dedication have paid off, literally. Some people question Mayweather's morals, or ridicule him for his arrogance, but it's hard to argue with his unparalleled achievements in boxing and the relentless dedication that backs it all up.

The best in the world are the best because they work their asses off doing what they were born to do. They make sacrifices. They keep grinding—and they don't stop.[36]

Byproducts Make You Bulletproof

I feel I have the authority to write this book because I've experienced a lot of the things I'm describing. I've quit my job to start something new. I've experienced the magic that happens at accelerator programs like TechStars. I've helped build a company from the ground up. I've seen my own startup produce millions of dollars and create jobs. I've toiled with the challenges of being a cofounder, and faced the harsh reality of failing at it.

My persistence led me through these experiences. There have been moments along my journey in which I've felt like an idiot, a loser, and an epic failure. But many of the decisions that resulted in failure were the same decisions that allowed me to meet amazing people, do amazing things, push my limits, and give me the insight and material to write this book. Through all of the stumbling, I was building up a base of knowledge, an arsenal of information that could then be molded into something unique and valuable.

This is the beauty of living with blind courage and testing the boundaries of your capability. Your relentless persistence will never be for naught. By taking the risks others won't take, you've given yourself an edge. You can sleep soundly at night, knowing valuable byproducts are constantly piling up behind you. You've already won.

---

36   http://en.wikipedia.org/wiki/Floyd_Mayweather,_Jr.

STEP 3: CREATE
PRODUCTIVITY AND EFFICIENCY

"Vision is not enough; it must be combined with venture. It is not enough to stare up the steps; we must step up the stairs."

VACLAV HAVEL

If you're brave enough to reject ZombieLand, and resilient enough to withstand multiple failures, you're ready for Step 3: Create. There's a vast ocean of things you could be working on, so I can't tell you exactly how to create whatever you're creating. But I *can* tell you how to set yourself up for success as you work through it. I'm talking about structuring the way you work, conditioning yourself to perform at the highest level, and eliminating common roadblocks. You don't have infinite money, resources, and time (nobody does), so you need to be efficient, effective, and productive in creation mode. Luckily, I know an expert who can help us with this. Say hello to Tim Ferriss.

Tim Ferriss and the Two Ps

Tim Ferriss is the author of the international bestseller, *The Four Hour Workweek*. He's also a lifehacker. He eliminates the parts of life that suck, and multiplies the parts that are awesome. He transforms impossible tasks into simple tasks. He turns fear into courage. He flips everything upside down. Tim is like Superman with an immunity to kryptonite.

Being Superman isn't all genetics, though. There's a lot of wizardry under his flashy red cape. It turns out that Tim is also a lot like the Wizard of Oz. He's able to produce seemingly impossible results using relatively simple tricks. His secret sauce is derived from two main principles:

1. The Pareto Principle
2. Parkinson's Law

The Pareto Principle, also known as the *80–20 rule*, or *the law of the vital few,* states that roughly 80% of the outcomes come from roughly 20% of the sources. To give some examples:

- 80% of your sales come from 20% of your clients
- 80% of your customer complaints come from 20% of your customers
- 80% of the world's wealth is owned by 20% of the population

The Pareto Principle crops up everywhere. In many cases, it's skewed even further (90-10, 95-5, 99-1). In the context of time and productivity, this means we need to focus on the biggest bang-for-buck activities, and avoid the biggest speed bumps. In the example of customer support, should you strive to answer every single inquiry, or should you ignore the small subset of customers who are generating the bulk of the complaints? Tim does the latter. Sometimes these decisions are hard to make, but they can dramatically improve efficiency.

The second ingredient in Tim's secret sauce, Parkinson's Law, states that the amount of work required to complete a task will expand or contract to fill the allotted time. Have you ever planned a social event and seen your friends fall into an endless state of "getting ready" until you tell them to stop? Eventually, you have to intervene and say, "Hey, it's time to go." This is Parkinson's Law in action. Your friends will continue fiddling with their hair or drinking their drinks until you force them to stop, because they're just filling the time. The takeaway here is that you must set constraints for yourself in order to stay productive. Otherwise, you'll just get drunk and mess with your hair all day.

Tim combines the Pareto Principle and Parkinson's Law to form the ultimate productivity hack:

1. Focus on the most important things
2. Set aggressive deadlines

Yep, that's it. It might sound simple, but we often struggle to execute it. It's far more difficult than it sounds. The chapters in this section are inspired by Pareto, Parkinson, and of course—Tim. It's a mixture of actionable advice, resources, and philosophical food-for-thought, focused on increasing productivity and efficiency. If all goes well, we'll have a bunch of Supermans and Wizards flying around pretty soon.

Time

10,000 Hours to Become an Expert?

Working on something meaningful will give you a sense of pride and put you in a better position to meet Connectors who share your passion. But ideally, you should become an *expert* in your craft, which can be daunting. Luckily, you don't need to spend as much time becoming an expert as you might think.

Malcolm Gladwell, in his bestselling book *Outliers*, popularized the theory that it takes 10,000 hours or more to become an expert in a cognitively demanding discipline.[37] He cites several relevant studies and examples, including the early career of the Beatles and the childhood of Bill Gates, to demonstrate the 10,000 hour rule in action.[38]

Naturally, a debate has formed around this topic. There have been numerous studies and articles written since the publishing of *Outliers*, most arguing that the 10,000 hour rule is faulty in some way. I've read a handful of these articles, and noticed that the vast majority attempt to refute Gladwell's claims by either debating the validity of the magic number (10,000 hours), or by arguing that innate talent, in addition to practice, plays a significant role in achieving expert-level success. But there's a third, often overlooked factor that I'd like to focus on instead. Namely—what is the task being learned?

---

37   http://tinyurl.com/mdsaq32

38   Credit should also be given to Anders Ericsson, a psychologist whose research on the same topic served as the foundation for Gladwell's theories.

To demonstrate the significance of this question, I'll tell you a quick story. In 2009, I found myself in a particularly deep pit of despair. I was getting seriously burnt out at work. The stress of being a cofounder was weighing on me. I was tired, unhealthy, and very unhappy. Battling insomnia, I would sometimes flip through infomercials late at night. One night, I came across P90X, a workout program on DVD. I purchased it on a whim. The package arrived a few days later and I decided to dedicate myself to it. I went through the program and gained thirty nine pounds of muscle in three months.

Exercise is now a staple in my life. At the time of this writing, I still do P90X, almost religiously. I know it like the back of my hand. I can do all the routines, performing each move in sequence without watching the DVDs.[39] Sometimes I even catch myself repeating Tony Horton's comments in my head before he says them. (He's the instructor). It's like knowing the lines of your favorite movie by heart. I've performed the moves so many times that they've been committed to memory. Not only that, I'm *good* at them. My form has been gradually perfected over the years. I would say I'm an expert at P90X, and I'm confident most people would agree.

Here's where this becomes relevant: If we look at this story in the context of the 10,000 hour rule, I beat the system. Or, you could say I found an exception. I didn't spend 10,000 hours practicing P90X. Not even close. The routines take an average of one hour per day, so that's 365 hours over

---

39   P90X consists of eleven different workouts, ranging from forty minutes to ninety minutes each.

the course of a year. My expert level was probably achieved after about two years, which would be 730 hours. But, I also took a long hiatus from the program after the initial three months. That drops it down to around 500 hours. So in my best estimate, it took me about 500 hours of intense practice to become an expert at P90X. Not 10,000 hours.

Does this mean Malcolm Gladwell's theory is wrong? No. I still believe practice and dedication, above anything else (God-given talent included), is the single biggest factor in achieving expert-level proficiency in a given discipline. Gladwell's theory still holds true, even in the face of my P90X example, because there's an important qualifier in his argument that most people miss: He isn't talking about *all* disciplines.

In *Outliers*, Gladwell examines difficult and nuanced tasks, such as playing the violin. He describes such tasks as *cognitively demanding*. So, he's making the argument that *cognitively demanding* disciplines require at least 10,000 hours of practice, not *all* disciplines. Logically then, it follows that the opposite is also true—that non-demanding disciplines do *not* require 10,000 hours of practice. This is precisely the case with P90X.

It took me only 500 hours to become an expert at P90X because:

1. P90X is *not cognitively demanding*.
2. P90X is *limited in scope*.

Not all disciplines are created equal. If I wanted to become an expert at tying my shoes (working on it), I bet I could achieve expert-level status after five solid hours of practice.

Conversely, if I wanted to become an expert at brain surgery, it would likely require 20,000 hours of practice at a minimum—well above Gladwell's magic number. The truth is that the magic number isn't a magic number at all, it's just a baseline for mastering really hard tasks. The amount of practice required to become an expert is relative to the difficulty and scope of the discipline.

Here's another secret: limiting the scope of your expertise is not only easier to achieve, *it's also far easier to apply in the real world.* To demonstrate: If I wanted to become a P90X trainer, I could. I could either train people individually or become a BeachBody coach.[40] I've achieved expert-level proficiency in P90X and can use it to my advantage. Not only is it a passion, it's also highly applicable to the social world in a way that could generate actual income and happiness for me. Because my knowledge is specific, it's easy to apply it to something actionable.

If I was trying to become an expert in something more broad, such as "health," it would not only take longer, it would also be more difficult to decide what to do with my vast knowledge once I had it. Should I become a personal trainer? A dietician? A doctor? A nutritionist? A massage therapist? A psychologist? These are all health-related professions. Too many choices.

Learn to narrow the scope of your expertise into something actionable. I don't need to be a health expert to teach P90X. I don't even need to be a weight-lifting expert. I just need to be a P90X expert. When you narrow the scope of

---

40   I was actually recruited by Tony Horton's sister to become a coach after emailing BeachBody about my body transformation.

your discipline, goals become more tangible. The work required becomes more manageable. Becoming an expert isn't as hard as you think. Forget 10,000 hours. Five-hundred is usually more than enough.

Let's look at one more example: Painting. Imagine that painting is your passion. What would you paint? Everything? Surely not. What are your specific interests? Landscapes? Abstracts? Anatomy? If you like anatomy, what kind? People? Animals? Okay, animals—great. What type? Horses? Perfect. Paint horses, and *only* horses. Paint horses in every position possible. Forget about everything else. No landscapes. No abstract art. No finger painting. Just horses.

For the sake of simplicity, let's say it takes ten hours to paint a really nice looking horse, and that it takes 100 attempts to become an expert at it. If you were practicing all kinds of other art styles and various subject matters, it might take you 10,000 hours to fit 100 horse paintings in. But by cutting everything else out, you can learn more efficiently, reaching expert-level status in the first 1,000 hours. As an added bonus, you'll actually enjoy what you're doing because you love horses! You no longer have to worry about the dreaded self-portraits and abstract art that were never really your thing. Here's the best part—after becoming an expert horse painter in record time, you'll find there's a healthy market for selling really amazing horse paintings. How do I know? Because there's always a market for really amazing things. Always. (You can re-read the section *Every Passion is Applicable* if you've forgotten.)

Have you ever noticed that famous painters are usually defined by a specific style and subject matter? For example, Claude Monet is an impressionist artist known for painting lily pads. This happens because the best artists have a narrow focus. They become obsessed with a particular subject matter, relentlessly honing their skill in that one specific area.

The Zone

Just as a narrow focus increases efficiency, so does a *heightened* focus. We've all experienced the Zone—a spark of inspiration followed by laser-sharp clarity and enhanced performance. It can strike in the middle of the night, on the toilet, or in the shower. Whenever you find yourself in the Zone, take advantage of it, because you can't come back to it later. The Zone comes and goes without warning.

Pay attention to the trigger(s) that put you in the Zone. My trigger is exercise. When I'm exercising, I'm usually hopped up on some kind of energy drink, my endorphins are surging, and my mind is clear. My very best ideas come to me in the middle of my workouts. When I realized this, I started exercising with my computer next to me. When the Zone struck, I'd immediately jump to my computer and start writing. Most of this book was drafted while I was half naked, sweaty as hell, and gasping for air.[41]

Not only did my best ideas come to me during my workouts, I was also able to produce content more rapidly. When in the Zone, I could write ten pages in twenty minutes. When out of the Zone, I would often stare at the screen for twenty minutes before writing a single sentence, or I'd procrastinate and work on other trivial tasks to fill the time.

---

41 Some of my other favorite triggers include the hot tub with an alcoholic beverage by my side (don't try this at home, kids), and the beach.

Knowing the trigger that puts you in the Zone allows you to build it into your routine. It turns out that exercise is more than just physical stimulation for me. It also triggers mental clarity, inspiration, and productivity. Because it's such a huge trigger, I try to exercise every day.

In sum, do this:

1. *Find your trigger.* When the Zone strikes, identify the trigger or circumstances that caused it.
2. *Prepare for the Zone.* Prior to engaging the trigger, gather whatever materials are necessary to be productive so you can jump into action as soon as the Zone hits.
3. *Build the trigger into your routine.* Schedule the trigger into your day to maximize your chances of experiencing the Zone consistently.

Productivity Hacks

"There's just not enough time in the day!" I've heard this statement—and felt this way—many, many times. The antithetical expression, *"I've got all the time in the world,"* is far more rare. How can we make the second statement the default? How can we get our time back?

First, let's take a moment to understand these expressions. In the first statement, "There's just not enough time in the day," we're really saying, "I spend the bulk of my day doing Y when I really want to be doing X." In the second statement, "I have all the time in the world," we're really saying, "I have a bunch of free time, so I fill it with X, which is what I love to do."

In scenario one, time has control over the person. In scenario two, the person has control over their time. Whenever you feel you have no time, there are two questions you need to ask:

1. What are all the things I'm currently doing?
2. What are the things I want to be doing instead of the things I'm doing?

Both questions are equally important. You must take note of all the things you're doing to determine whether or not you need to keep doing them, but you must also determine what you will do after you've freed up additional time. Otherwise, you'll end up staring blankly at a wall. Remember, the opposite of happiness is boredom. Dead time is just as torturous as a lack of free time.

After rejecting ZombieLand and committing to a specific project or goal (which naturally answers the second question above), most people realize they can remove low-value activities to make room for high-value activities that fuel their purpose. Here's a list of low-value activities I've either reduced considerably, or removed completely from my schedule:

1. Email
2. TV
3. Paying bills
4. Talking on the phone
5. Texting/chatting
6. Commuting/driving
7. Cooking

8. Errands/Chores
9. Shopping
10. Favors
11. Worrying
12. Browsing the internet
13. Reading /watching the news
14. Researching
15. Social networking

I've compiled some tips on how to fight back against these common time-wasters. Included with the tips are a bunch of services that might also help. I've used most of these services myself. You should consider these lists a starting point. Be sure to explore the services yourself and look for alternatives. New and innovative products are being launched every day.

Email

I've reduced my time spent on email by 95%, from roughly twenty hours per week to one hour per week. Here's how to do it (hat tip to Tim Ferriss on this topic):

- *Cancel all subscriptions and notifications.* No more newsletters or daily deals.
- *Don't give out your email to third party sites.* Create a secondary account for signing up for new services. This significantly reduces spam.
- *For close contacts, respond to open ended emails with a phone call whenever possible.* Phone calls are more personable, and it's easier to get things done more

quickly. You'll also find that most people don't pick up, which is great. Leave a message. Done.[42]

- *Schedule a time to check email once or twice (no more than twice) per day for ten minutes.* When you start, set a timer. When the ten minutes are up, you're done. The rest can wait until tomorrow. When the time is up, be sure to close your email client. Leaving it open will be too tempting. Turn off email notifications on your phone, as well.[43]

You'll find that a lot of catch-up can be done on Saturdays. Don't check email on Sundays, if possible. If, after using these methods, your email is still piling up, consider outsourcing some of your email to an assistant. You can find virtual assistants (VA's) for as little as $5 per hour.[44]

---

42   If you must write a long email to someone close to you, it's okay. I don't classify this as email. I consider it valuable time spent communicating with someone you care about. When this happens, I usually write the message in a text editor (outside of my email client) to separate it from the activity of email. I define the process of email as:

1. Reviewing incoming messages
2. Responding to non-personal contacts

Note that if you make a phone call in this situation, it's *your* choice, not the other person's choice. This is important because it keeps the communication on your terms.

43   You may want to skip this if you're expecting important emails. Sometimes I leave email notifications activated on my mobile device, but I make an effort to stay disciplined. I only view an email if it looks personal or urgent. Otherwise, I wait until the next scheduled review period.

44   There's a full section about VA's in The *Four Hour Workweek* by Tim Ferriss.

If a VA is processing your email for an hour a day at $5 per hour, the cost is about $150 per month. This should cut your workload considerably, and make your personal commitment of ten minutes per day more than manageable.[45] If you're like me, you've just reduced time spent on email from twenty hours per week to one hour per week, a 95% reduction. You've gained nineteen hours per week, or roughly seventy-five hours per month. If you're using a VA and want to look at the cost-to-benefit ratio of this in terms of expenses, you're getting an additional seventy-five hours of free time per month for a cost of $150. That's $2 per hour of free time. Is your time worth more than $2 per hour? I would hope so.

Note that this method is easily customizable. For example, you can decide to check email regularly on Mondays, Wednesdays, and Fridays, and use the ten minute rule only on Tuesdays, Thursdays, and Saturdays. You can also adjust the ten minute rule to twenty minutes, etc.

To close out this section, the two most important steps in reducing time spent on email are:

1. Remove lengthy back-and-forth communication.
2. Block out a specific time to check email so you're not doing it constantly throughout the day.

---

45 By compartmentalizing email, I haven't needed to use a Virtual Assistant, although I have a friend who hired one, and he highly recommends it.

TV

Avoid live programming. Use that magical doo-hicky called a DVR to record your favorite programs and watch them later (or use Netflix, or Hulu). You should do this for two reasons:

1. It allows you to take downtime on *your* schedule, not the schedule of a television network.
2. It allows you to skip commercials, which can reduce time spent by 30-50%.

As a general rule, just don't watch TV. Ninety-nine percent of it is garbage. Don't leave the TV on in the background or channel-surf either, unless you're spending your time that way deliberately (i.e. "It's Sunday and I'm vegging out!"). If you really want to watch specific TV shows, try to hold yourself to one or two, at most. Anything beyond that will start to dominate your schedule. Passive entertainment can be a great stress-reducing activity, but keep it in check and don't let it become a daily habit.

Paying Bills

Set up autopay. Check your bank statements monthly for any strange or unexpected charges. Done.

Answering the Phone

Don't do it, unless it's a close contact. Screen calls. Set a time to check voicemail. Get back to people on your own time. Get your voicemail transcribed so you can view it in text form and respond by text or email.

Voicemail Transcription Services:
- Grasshopper: http://grasshopper.com/
- Libon: https://www.libon.com/

Texting/Chatting
See above.

Commuting/Driving
Don't do it. Live as close to work as possible, or work remotely if you can. Use commuting as an excuse to work from home if possible.[46]

Cooking
Here are some services that can make cooking more efficient, or remove it from your plate completely (food pun!):

Get groceries delivered to your door.
- Instacart: https://www.instacart.com/store
- AmazonFresh:[47] https://fresh.amazon.com

Get ingredients for pre-determined meals delivered to your door.
- Blue Apron: http://www.blueapron.com/
- Plated: http://www.plated.com/
- PlateJoy: http://www.platejoy.com/
- Forage: http://www.forage.co/

---

46   See *The Four Hour Workweek* by Tim Ferriss, and *Remote* by Jason Fried and David Heinemeier Hansson, for a lot more on the topic of working remotely.

47   Only available in select areas at the time of this writing.

Get pre-cooked meals delivered to your door.
- FreshDiet: http://www.thefreshdiet.com/
- SpoonRocket: https://www.spoonrocket.com/
- Munchery: https://munchery.com/

Pre-cooked meal services can be a little expensive, so only do this if you have the available funds. I used FreshDiet for years, and it was a huge time-saver.

Errands/Chores

There are plenty of services that can speed up or erase chores and errands for a reasonable price. Check out these awesome services for taking care of general tasks, shipping stuff, cleaning, and handyman work:
- TaskRabbit: https://www.taskrabbit.com/
- HomeJoy: https://www.homejoy.com/
- GetMaid: http://getmaid.com/[48]
- Handy: http://www.handybook.com/
- Shyp: http://www.shyp.com/

Shopping

Shop Online.[49]
- Amazon: http://www.amazon.com/
- Overstock: http://www.overstock.com/
- Craigslist: http://www.craigslist.org/

---

48   Currently only available in NYC.
49   I know this is obvious to some. You'd be surprised how many people still wait in lines at the mall.

I recommend getting Amazon Prime. For an annual fee, you get free two-day shipping on all orders.[50] I have Amazon Prime and it usually pays for itself within a few months. Imagine buying a book or new workout gear and having to wait two weeks before it arrives. That waiting period can kill your motivation and momentum. Prime gets it to your doorstep in forty-eight hours.

If you must shop offline, outsource it whenever possible with TaskRabbit or a similar service (https://www.taskrabbit.com/). Finally, stop shopping so much. You probably don't need 90% of the things you're buying.

Favors

Don't do them as often. When you do a favor, do it consciously and deliberately because you want to. Don't do it out of guilt or an unspoken obligation. Do big favors only for close friends. They should be in your inner circle. Help secondary contacts and strangers as well, but only as your schedule permits.

Worrying

Worrying is not useful. This is a tough one. I'm constantly working on this, and you should too. When you realize you're worrying, accept it. Then consciously clear it out of your mind. Writing it down and setting it aside sometimes helps. Your mind will stop focusing on it, knowing it's stored safely somewhere else. Come back to your worry list once per week and ask yourself if the items on your list

---

50   With Amazon Prime, you also get some other perks, like the ability to live-stream Amazon's entire movie library for no additional cost.

really matter or not. If they do, leave them there. If not, cross them off.

Browsing the Internet

Check out RescueTime. It's a software tool that tracks your browsing activity and helps you avoid distractions. If you deliberately browse for fun in your free time, that's fine.

- RescueTime: https://www.rescuetime.com/

Reading/Watching the News

I consider this a complete waste of time. I don't do it. If anything important happens, I'll hear about it. If I haven't heard about it, it's not important.

I use a feed reader to read only the blogs I find useful. I also occasionally use an app called Circa. Matt Galligan, a fellow TechStars alum, is Circa's founder and CEO. He describes the product as *"cliff notes for news."* It's great because you can quickly catch up on only the stories you care about. If you want to stay informed on a particular story, you can follow it with the tap of a button, and you'll get updates as related information becomes available. Circa writes its own articles, so all of the content is fresh and original. It's like a feed within a feed, in snackable form. Fantastic.

Researching

Researching usually involves comparing two or more similar things, either for depth of knowledge, or to determine the best option. Research of this kind has diminishing returns. Usually the first hour is more valuable than however many hours follow it—by an order of magnitude. The most important information is easy to find. The rest doesn't matter much. When I'm researching something, I limit myself to 2-5 sources. Anything beyond that likely won't contribute substantially to what's already been found.

You'll never be 100% informed. Realize that the most important information is the easiest to find, and concede that you'll never know everything there is to know. It's okay.

Social Networking

Don't waste time scanning your Facebook feed. If you want to follow up with important people in your life, make a filter to only show those people. This will save you from 'Facebook feed creep,' the horribly addicting act of scrolling endlessly through your feed, looking at posts from people you don't really care about. Why are you doing this? Get back to doing something meaningful.[51]

Using a Feed Reader

Being able to synthesize a bunch of information on a given topic is useful, but it can also be time consuming. First, you need to do preliminary research to find good sources of information. Then, you need to constantly revisit those sources to see if any new content has been posted since the last time you checked. News apps like Circa are starting to fix this problem. Feed Readers (also referred to as RSS Feeds, or content aggregators) also provide a robust solution. *If you already use a feed reader, feel free to skip this section.*

---

51 Remember that this activity also exposes you to the Generalized Friend Paradox. It will likely make you feel sorry for yourself if you do it too frequently.

Feed readers allow you to subscribe to nearly any website. After subscribing to sites of interest, any new content published to those sites will automatically flow into your feed reader. The content is displayed in an easy-to-read format, without any advertisements or other visual distractions.

Feed readers have had a long and bumpy history. Several old feed readers, such as Google Reader, are now defunct, but new products have filled the void. I currently use a very effective feed reader called Feedly. I've organized my feeds into the following custom categories: Sports, Technology, and Other Stuff.

In the Sports section, I subscribe to a popular college sports blog that covers University of Michigan sports exclusively, because I'm a Michigan sports addict. The stories come directly into Feedly, so I never miss a post. I've been to the blog's website, and it's an eyesore. In Feedly, I don't have to worry about that. It strips away the design so I can view just the text on a blank white background, like a page in a book.

In the Technology section, I subscribe to popular tech blogs like *TechCrunch* and *VentureBeat*. I also subscribe to the blogs of various VCs and startup gurus whom I admire. This is my largest section, with nearly twenty feeds.

In the Other Stuff section, I subscribe to a handful of thought leaders who write primarily about lifestyle design. This section includes the blogs of Tim Ferriss, Leo Babauta, and *The Minimalists*. These sources give me inspiration, and also serve as a nice mental break from work whenever I need it.

At any given time, I'm usually subscribed to between 20-30 sites from across the web. This becomes my information hub. I don't need to enter a bunch of URLs or search Google for new content. I simply open my feed reader. Having the fresh content at my fingertips saves an enormous amount of time. It streamlines my information-gathering and gives me a constant flow of new material for inspiration and ideas. Notice that I don't subscribe to CNN or ESPN. That's because these sources are too broad. I instead look for very specific sources that give me rich, focused material.

Feedly has keyboard shortcuts on the desktop version, and clever swiping gestures on the mobile version for even quicker consumption. I view articles in the *Titles Only* view, which shows only headlines. I can click any headline to view the full story. I usually scan through hundreds of stories a day in this format, reading the 15-20 that look the most intriguing. I check Feedly a few times a day, about twenty minutes per session. When people mention recent news happening in the startup world, I usually already know about it.

A word of advice—if you start using a feed reader like Feedly, be wary of adding too many sources or subscribing to sites that post too frequently. You might experience content overload, which can get overwhelming in a hurry. If you're spending hours scanning your feeds every day, consider removing a few sources to lighten the load.

To take your information synthesis to the next level, save your favorite posts to services like Evernote, Pocket, or Instapaper. These services store content so you can easily review it later. I use Pocket for saving my favorite articles, and Evernote for taking general notes on anything that comes to mind. In Pocket, I tag content as much as possible so it can be easily filtered in the future. How do you think

I kept my research organized for this book? Every article with relevant content was stored in Pocket and tagged as *Book Material*.

- Evernote: www.evernote.com
- Pocket: www.getpocket.com
- Instapaper: www.instapaper.com/

Focus Time

Most people put appointments on their calendar. Meeting @6pm. Deadline @2pm. This is fine, but you should also block out time on your schedule specifically for uninterrupted focus time. This is time to be spent on whatever project you like. Commit to *not* doing anything else during that time. No phone calls, no texts, no emails, no meetings. This can be done in both personal and work settings.

Too often, we allow other people to interrupt our flow. We feel obligated to answer our phones, respond to texts, and constantly check our email. If you want to get things done, you need to consciously resist these urges. Just because technology makes us perpetually accessible doesn't mean we should be on call to everyone, everywhere, all the time. That's absurd.

You can be most productive when the world is asleep. The early morning hours are best for me. That's when I feel the most creative and energetic. In my late twenties, I would wake consistently at 5 a.m. Lately, it's closer to 7 a.m. If you're a night owl, working at night may suit you better. Experiment with it, but find a block of time when everyone else is snoozing. The absence of interruption is arguably the most effective productivity enhancer.

Be Short-Sighted

Believe it or not, being short-sighted is more efficient than planning ahead. Don't think too much about the long-term effect of a particular decision, and don't try to map out every detail of your career. It's easier to execute precisely on a two week plan versus a two year plan. You should have a long-term vision in mind, but don't dwell on it. Trying to consider every possible outcome and plan contingencies can cause paralysis of analysis—one of the most common excuses for staying in ZombieLand.

Long-term goals also tend to distract you from enjoying your life *right now*. When only long-term goals are motivating you, weeks turn into months, and months turn into years. It's easy to lose track of yourself, your time, and what you really want. Contrast this with being short-sighted and living in small batches—one to two week chunks. With a short-sighted mentality, you're still working toward bigger milestones, but you're constantly evaluating your current situation and your direction. It keeps you more agile and more present. Instead of writing plans all day, you'll be getting things done and reviewing the results.

Eric Ries describes the benefits of small-batching in his bestseller, *The Lean Startup*. If you have a large stack of envelopes to stuff, seal, and stamp, the common approach is to batch out the process. That is, you would first fold all the papers, then stuff all the envelopes, then seal all the envelopes, then stamp them. Surprisingly, the more efficient process is to complete the steps for each envelope, one at a time. Ries explains:

Why does stuffing one envelope at a time get the job done faster even though it seems like it would be slower? Because our intuition doesn't take into account the extra time required to sort, stack, and move around the large piles of half-complete envelopes when it's done the other way.

Convention tells us to plan and batch out our lives, but it actually slows us down. Small-batching keeps us more nimble. Broad-batching also leaves us vulnerable to traveling down the wrong path for an incredibly long time before uncovering a problem, while small-batching reveals problems immediately. Ries again provides insight:

> Even if the amount of time that each process took was exactly the same, the small-batch production approach still would be superior, and for even more counterintuitive reasons. For example, imagine that the letters didn't fit in the envelopes. With the large-batch approach, we wouldn't find that out until nearly the end. With small batches, we'd know almost immediately. What if the envelopes are defective and won't seal? In the large-batch approach, we'd have to unstuff all the envelopes, get new ones, and re-stuff them. In the small-batch approach, we'd find this out immediately and have no re-work required.[52]

---

52   Eric Ries, *The Lean Startup: How Today's Entrepreneurs Use Continuous Innovation to Create Radically Successful Businesses.* (Crown Business 2011).

Consider this in the context of your life or career. Is it useful to introduce yourself to 10,000 people you think are important? Or, would it be more useful to build solid relationships with a select few? Should you dabble in 10,000 different activities, hoping to eventually create something of value? Or should you focus on a specific discipline that peaks your interest, and figure out if you can become the best at it? Would it be smart to build out the entire infrastructure for your latest product? Or, would it be smarter to get a lightweight prototype into a few hands to gauge interest and uncover potential issues?

Forget about long-term goals and plans. Forget about batching your life. Being short-sighted is the most efficient way to get things done. You'll accomplish tasks more quickly, avoid costly mistakes, and ensure you're enjoying yourself *right now*.

Linear Is Dumb

People who do things out of order and without permission get more done, faster. Can you make progress toward fulfilling a Passion Arc *right now*? You probably can. Your life doesn't have to follow a linear progression. In fact, it shouldn't.

Mark Zuckerberg, the CEO and founder of Facebook, didn't ask for permission to get started. He began experimenting and building products while he was still enrolled at Harvard. Even before Facebook, he built a service called FaceMash. Zuckerberg is now one of the most respected CEOs in the country—and one of the youngest. He fast-tracked his life by doing things out of order—by not waiting in line.

Early in Facebook's history, Zuckerberg developed a mantra that was derived from his own habits. The mantra is plastered throughout his company's offices. *Move fast and break things.* Zuckerberg comes from a hacker background. This doesn't mean he breaks into banks. It means he questions conventional thinking and finds better solutions through constant experimentation. He understands the benefit of exploration, of moving quickly, of taking *action.* This is how innovation happens.[53]

What if you didn't have to wait in line? What if you could break the rules and skip ahead? What if *there was no line*?

Work Journal #4: The Subway

Circa 2006, Written at Work

The worst invention in New York City is the subway system. Yeah, it gets you from point A to point B, but only at the expense of your dignity.

Before I walk into the subway, I always take a deep breath and let out a sigh. I have to mentally prepare myself for the inhumane jungle of frantic sheep that I'm

---

53   While this book was being written, Zuckerberg made some comments at his annual F8 conference, implying that the mantra no longer held. He said, "We used to have this mantra, 'Move fast and break things.' We were willing to tolerate a few bugs to [move fast]. But having to slow down and fix things was slowing us down. 'Move fast with stable infra[structure]' isn't as catchy, but it helps us build better for the people we serve." This is an important point. Don't move *too* fast or things can fall apart, and be sure you're working from a strong foundation. (http://tinyurl.com/nj3kcqf)

about to enter. I also take a deep breath because it will be my last breath of fresh air for a while.

The subway experience first assaults me through the nose. The smell of stale urine fills my nostrils from all angles. There are pools of it lurking everywhere. It could be the puddle in front of my feet, or the spot of dried up composted trash caked on the wall, or both. It could even be that man in the corner wearing a huge winter coat but no shoes, munching the end of an old McDonalds french fry container and frantically mumbling to himself on the floor. He's saying something about how the world is going to end.

The best part though, is the visual chaos—the deluge of people running around, trying to figure out where they are and what they are doing. They act as if the world will end if they don't squeeze themselves into the train car before the doors shut.

The platform is eerily silent as the train zips off into the endless underground tunnels. Five minutes later, more sheep file in and the process repeats.

The trains, which also smell of urine, crash against the tracks as if they might veer off at any moment, smashing into the concrete walls and bursting into a fireworks display of sparks and metal. The entire train heaves back and forth at certain junctures, jolting everyone inside against each other.

Describing the train as crowded is an understatement. We're packed in like play-doh. On most days, my face is about two inches from four other faces, my hand is grasping a greasy pole along with ten other hands, my crotch is three inches away from someone's face, and my ass is touching someone else's face. It's fantastically horrible.

When everything feels like a drag, you should stop and ask yourself, *"Why?"* Why are you in this situation? You'll quickly realize that you have deeper problems than whatever is currently pissing you off. Although it doesn't take up physical space, the "drag" takes up mental space. It saps your motivation and literally slows you down. To be truly productive—to get inspired and hit the Zone, you need to remove the drag.

Quit Your Job

There are plenty of tips and tricks for increasing productivity, but those are the 80% of changes that contribute to 20% of your results. To find the other 20% of changes that will contribute to 80% of your results, we need to look at *big* changes. Simply put, the best way to get more done faster is to fill your schedule with less. When you're working on a big project, things like email, errands, and housework, get in the way. Reducing them helps. But the real culprit is your boring job. If you're spending 40+ hours per week at the office, your ability to make progress on your passion is significantly limited. If you really want to go all in, you need extreme focus. You need to quit.

If this sounds crazy—it should. Cutting off income will be a shock to your system. It creates a countdown clock you can't possibly ignore. With no cash coming in, you *must* build an income-generating product before running out of funds. Welcome to the startup game. Quitting your job lets you focus 100% on your project, and gives you a tangible, hard deadline. It's the productivity hack at its best. Remember: *Extreme Focus + Aggressive Deadlines = Ultra Productivity.*

Saving up enough money to cut off income isn't as hard as it sounds. If you plan for it and manage your living expenses carefully, it's doable for anyone with a middle-range income or higher. I know plenty of friends who had more money in the bank than I did when I refused to get a job so I could write this book. And those friends never sold a company or won the lottery. They weren't even pulling in six-figure salaries. Nope, they just saved their money over time. When I left my company, I had funds to last about a year. If I had never started my own company, and I had remained at my previous job in New York City, I would have had nearly the same savings, just by putting some cash away each month.

In business, the MVP isn't the Most Valuable Player, it's the *Minimum Viable Product.* It's the most bare-bones version of whatever you're trying to sell. After creating an MVP, you can often raise additional funding through angel investors, crowdfunding platforms, venture capitalists, or banks. Completing an MVP can usually be accomplished in 3-6 months (or less) with the proper planning and focus.

This is, in fact, the exact model of most startup accelerator programs. When I joined TechStars, our team of two people (myself and my partner) received a check for $10,000. We had three months to make something happen, and we did. How long would it take you to save up $10,000? With a mid-range income, you should be able to do it in less than a year. Accelerator programs are much more competitive these days, and most programs offer more funding and accept more mature companies, but you don't necessarily need to be in a program to accelerate your progress. You just need the formula: Clear your schedule and create a deadline. Quitting your job fulfills both objectives. 10K won't last very long these days, but a budget of 30-50K should be more than enough to drop your job and create your MVP.[54] If you're young and unencumbered, you can get away with far less. Saving $1,000 a month gets you to 30K in just a few years. If you have a partner in crime, you're there in less than eighteen months.

Don't work to live. Live to work. Throw away your 9-5 for a while and focus on the project you love. The worst case scenario is going back to your 9-5 if your MVP flops— and if you're worried about that outcome, ZombieLand has strangled you and you're already dead.

Earn Cash, Get Funded, & Launch Your Project

It's never been easier to fund personal projects, create supplemental income, and launch new companies. There are countless resources to help you raise money and find support for your project, especially after you've already built an MVP. There are also numerous ways to pad your bank account with extra cash to extend your runway. The sharing economy, accelerator programs, and crowdfunding

---

54   You may need more if you have a family to support, or other financial obligations, or a capital intensive business idea. The cost-of-living in your particular location is also a factor. The figures I'm presenting are ballparks.

companies are leading this revolution. Below is a list of resources you might find helpful. I've used many of these resources myself. This list isn't exhaustive, but it's a good place to start.

Accelerate Your Company

Accelerators have become one of the best ways to fund a new company.[55] The top programs are extremely competitive, but if you can put together an all-star team or build a product that gets initial traction, you'll have a shot at getting accepted. Each program is different. Do your research before applying.

- TechStars: http://www.techstars.com/
- YCombinator: http://ycombinator.com/
- 500 Startups: http://500.co/
- AngelPad: http://angelpad.org/
- DreamIt Ventures: http://www.dreamitventures.com/
- Seed-DB: This is a database of accelerator programs. At the time of this writing, the site lists over 200 programs, which can be sorted and filtered across several useful metrics. http://www.seed-db.com/accelerators

Earn Supplemental Income on the Side

The sharing economy is creating new ways for people to

---

55   Accelerators typically offer some type of funding at the onset, but the true value lies in the mentorship, publicity, and subsequent connections that are made by virtue of being in the program itself. Most programs culminate in a demo day—a live event where companies pitch themselves to investors. The access to mentors and investors gives incubated companies a considerable edge over non-incubated companies.

earn supplemental income from the stuff they already own. Top performers make a healthy living from these services, often quitting their day jobs.

Rent out your home.
- AirBNB: https://www.airbnb.com/[56]

Rent out your car.
- Getaround: https://www.getaround.com/
- Relay Rides: https://relayrides.com/

Rent out your bike.
- Splinster: https://www.spinlister.com/

Give people a ride using your own vehicle.
- Lyft: http://www.lyft.com/
- Uber: https://www.uber.com/

Sell handmade goods.
- Etsy: https://www.etsy.com/

Do simple tasks for others.
- TaskRabbit: https://www.taskrabbit.com/

---

56   I used AirBNB frequently while writing this book, renting out my Santa Monica apartment to earn over $15,000 in passive income. When the apartment was being rented, I'd stay with local friends or find cheap flights and travel domestically. I was making money while taking trips to amazing cities like San Diego and New York City. And, of course, my free time was still 100% preserved, so I could keep making progress on the book.

Dog sit.
- DogVacay: http://dogvacay.com/

Do handyman, house cleaning, and outdoor work.
- Zaarly: https://www.zaarly.com/

Sell or rent your clothes (women's clothing only, for now).
- Poshmark: https://poshmark.com/

Sell absolutely anything.
- Craigslist: http://www.craigslist.org/

Create your own eCommerce store.
- Shopify: http://www.shopify.com/

Raise Money for your Company or Project

Raising capital used to be tough. The main funding sources were banks or venture capitalists. Today, there are a myriad of options for funding your company, or anything else you might be working on. Most of the services below are crowd-funding platforms. In the crowdfunding model, anyone can pledge money to fund your project. Crowdfunding is a great way to build an audience while simultaneously raising money. It's sales, marketing, and fundraising wrapped into one.

Raise money for anything.
- Indiegogo: https://www.indiegogo.com/
- Kickstarter: https://www.kickstarter.com/[57]

---

57   I used Kickstarter to raise funds for this book.

Raise money for your book, or self publish it.
- Unbound: http://unbound.co.uk/
- Lulu: http://www.lulu.com/

Raise money for anything, in exchange for a small portion of any income you make in the future.
- Upstart: https://www.upstart.com/

There are also business-specific crowdfunding platforms:
- Fundable: http://www.fundable.com/
- Crowdfunder:https://www.crowdfunder.com/
- Funder's Club: https://fundersclub.com/
- AngelList: https://angel.co/

Many of the services in this section are highly competitive. You'll need a compelling story, an impressive track record, or a high performing MVP to give yourself a chance at getting accepted. If you're raising money to start a company, you should also find at least one cofounder. The likelihood of getting funded as a solitary founder is low. Why? Because running a business is lonely and stressful. The best support comes from cofounders who are battling alongside you. Investors know the importance of this, and the increased likelihood of failure without it.

Meng To's Creation

Remember our Cambodian friend, Meng To? Well, he didn't need to use the fundraising approach. He went straight to making money. Meng learned a lot about Sketch (the design program similar to Photoshop) by using it for all of his side projects. Eventually, he started writing blog posts about it. The posts spread like wildfire, attracting millions of views from designers all over the world. People were dying to know more, and they loved Meng's teaching style. It was simple and direct.

So, over the course of about six months, he compiled his knowledge into a digital book, which he titled *Design+Code*. It was meant to teach designers and programmers how to build apps using Sketch and a bit of code. But it's much more than a book. It's fourteen years of Meng's design knowledge, in the form of videos, tutorials, and prose. Meng treats it as a SAAS (Software as a Service) product, making frequent updates and providing ongoing support to his customers. The book was downloaded over 7,000 times within the first six months of its release, which translated into hundreds of thousands of dollars being deposited in Meng's bank account. After years of failed experiments, he had finally found his income-generating Purpose Spurt.[58]

Time Is NOT Money

Speaking of bank accounts, imagine a bank account that holds all of your monetary assets. This account is peculiar, though. It has a policy that you *must* withdraw the same amount of cash each day until your balance reaches zero. You're not allowed to deposit additional funds into the account. You're only permitted to spend down from the original balance.

---

58 Note that this is a perfect demonstration of "Making money from anything." Meng packages his unique knowledge and sells it—and his customers are extremely happy with the value he delivers.

Regardless of what you spend the money on, the same relatively small portion must be removed each day. You can't take the money out and save it somewhere else, and you must spend it on the day it's withdrawn. By the way, there's no telling when this bank might shut down—and if it shuts down before your balance reaches zero, the remaining funds will no longer be available.

Lousy bank, right? That's because it isn't actually a bank. It's your life. The funds in the account represent the days you have left to live. Knowing that *time*—one of your most valuable currencies—is diminishing at a constant rate, don't you want to make good use of it? What would you spend your time on *right now*, knowing you might not have access to it five years from now, or one year from now, or one *month* from now?

Time is not money. Time is *everything*. It's the single most important asset we have, and one of only two basic assets that really matter in life. The other is health.

Body

Take Care of Your Temple

Our body is our vehicle for getting things done. Without it, we're useless. For most of us, brushing our teeth and showering have their place on the daily routine list—but for some reason, things like sleeping, eating properly, and exercising, tend to fall off the radar.

When I worked at SeamlessWeb (now known as Seamless), I was young and scrappy. It was my first job out of college. I would get into work early, around 7:30 or 8 a.m.

My job was to speak to local restaurants in Manhattan and convince them to join the SeamlessWeb network. I had to set up meetings over the phone and then travel around the city to deliver my pitch to the owners in person. I usually spent the early mornings making calls and confirming appointments. I'd schedule a set of morning meetings and a set of afternoon meetings. For lunch, I'd come back to the office to catch up on email (this was before smartphones existed.)

My lunch was always the same: A Cup O' Noodles.[59] I could add hot water from the watercooler and it was ready to eat in seconds. I chose the Cup O' Noodles as my meal for two reasons:

1. It was quick and easy to make
2. It was cheap (I think around sixty cents)

I didn't have much money at the time, and I wanted to squeeze as many meetings into my day as possible. The Cup O' Noodles was the perfect solution.

After a few months on the job, the lead sales guy—we'll call him Jeff (not his real name), invited me to lunch. At first, I wasn't sure what to do. I knew it would be far more expensive than my usual meal, and it would probably disrupt my schedule for the day. On the other hand, Jeff had a great reputation at the company and seemed like a nice guy, so I was interested in getting to know him.

I reluctantly accepted his invitation and we went to a deli around the corner. Jeff said they had amazing sandwiches. I ordered a tuna melt. It was huge and I could hardly finish it,

---

59   A styrofoam cup filled with dry ramen noodles.

but it was delicious. It took 15-20 minutes to get our food, and we spent another forty minutes eating and talking, mostly about how I was adapting to my new position. Toward the end of the meal, I was feeling antsy. I had spent a considerable amount of time and money meeting with Jeff, but I hadn't gotten much out of it. At the risk of sounding like a jerk, I asked why he invited me.

"So why did we come to lunch today?" I asked. "Did you have any advice for me?"

"This lunch *is* the advice," he replied.

I didn't understand. "What do you mean?"

"You have to take care of your temple," he said, gesturing at his body. "I've seen you running into the office to eat your ramen noodles every day and then rushing back out. That's not sustainable. You'll run out of gas. You have to take care of your body, take a break every once in a while, enjoy a good meal. This isn't a sprint, it's a marathon."

"Okay," I said. "That's a good point. Thanks."

After Jeff's explanation, I was embarrassed. Clearly, everyone in the office had noticed my peculiar lunch routine, and Jeff was calling me out on it. Did it really matter? As it turns out, it *did*—a lot.

For the next few weeks, I took longer lunches and ate bigger meals. My productivity at work didn't go down. To my surprise, it shot way up. Although I was spending more time and money on lunch, I was performing better. I was able to close more deals, and sometimes even schedule more meetings, because I had more energy. I also found that eating lunch at a target restaurant before the meeting was an effective selling strategy. By eating their food (which was sometimes expensive), I was demonstrating my confidence in their product. The owners usually tried to comp the meals, but I'd refuse. It was against our company policy—and besides, spending my own money on a good meal made me look more legitimate.

When you're hustling, it's easy to push your health aside, but taking care of your body is a key ingredient in being productive and effective in your work. Eating a good meal shouldn't feel like an obstacle in the middle of your day. It should feel like a well-deserved recharging session. Always take care of your temple. Don't neglect it.

Why Exercise Is Everything

It may seem strange to dedicate an entire section of the book to the condition of your body. The Connection Algorithm is about taking risks and living through passion—so, why are we talking about eating healthy and doing push-ups? Believe it or not, it's an integral piece of the puzzle. I didn't realize it (or maybe I just deliberately ignored it) until I was nearly thirty, but your body and your health are inextricably intertwined with your performance and success. The process of exercising is also a metaphorical template for the entire lifestyle I'm preaching about. Specifically:

1. Push Your Comfort Zone
2. Create Constraints
3. Persist
4. Get an Edge

Push Your Comfort Zone

When you exercise, you're pushing your body to its physical limits. You're straining your muscles, which causes them to grow. The experience is uncomfortable. It's painful, but it's the struggle that garners results. This is the same struggle we face as founders, leaders, and innovators. Getting outside of your comfort zone is the only way to achieve significant growth.

Create Constraints

When I integrated P90X into my life, both the program and my daily schedule created important constraints. The program itself was designed to be completed in ninety days, which gave me clear milestones and an attainable finish line.[60] My existing routine forced me to exercise in the mornings, which kept me disciplined. (If I didn't workout right away, it might never happen, so I had to do it immediately after waking up.) Constraints should be integrated into as many areas of your life as possible. They provide structure, and force you to perform.

Persist

The inherent constraints of P90X demanded a patterned behavior, which quickly formed into a habit. After the first month, I was waking up at 5 a.m. without a problem, eating more, and seeing results. With each passing day, it became more important to maintain my streak—to make it through the ninety days without lapsing. The constant and consistent grind helped me stay focused on the end goal.

---

60   Even though the ninetieth day was considered the finish line, I didn't see it as the ultimate end. It was just another milestone. I wanted the habit of exercise to become a part of my life, so I mentally prepared myself to keep doing P90X after day ninety.

Get an Edge

My decision to explore P90X definitely gave me an edge in terms of my health. A recent study revealed that only 5% of the population engages in physical activity at least once per day.[61] I exercise for about an hour a day, so I'm in the top 5%, and most likely in the top 1-2%, given the strenuous nature of P90X.

Keep in mind, P90X isn't the only option. Other people join running groups, play recreational sports, hire personal coaches, train for marathons, take yoga classes, or join gyms. Those are all great options, too. The important element is the patterned behavior. Find your optimal system for getting an edge, and repeat it consistently. It's necessary—both in health and in life—if you wish to reach your full potential. It's not that hard to get into a groove. You just have to work it into your daily routine—like showering, or brushing your teeth.

The Edge

The concept of the Edge is important. The Edge is the extra ounce of effort needed to get ahead of the pack, to put yourself in the top five percent. It isn't exclusive to health. It applies to everything. Examples include:

- Having a better product than 95% of the competition
- Working harder than 95% of your co-workers
- Being more informed than 95% of your peers

---

61   http://tinyurl.com/26jua9l

The common expressions "going the extra mile" and "the icing on the cake" describe the Edge. Most people don't realize:

1. How much of an impact The Edge has on success
2. How easy it is to achieve

There is often very little separating average and extraordinary people. Most of us are lazy. To be extraordinary, you just have to be a little less lazy than everyone else.

Getting the Edge is a mindset, and exercising happens to be a great way to train yourself into that mindset. When we exercise, we naturally seek the Edge, because our performance is measured. We measure the weight we lift, the number of repetitions we complete in sequence, the distance and speed of our running and swimming, the duration of time we can hold a yoga pose, etc. These measurements then allow us to push for the extra mile. If we did eight reps last week, we shoot for nine the following week.

In life, most of us don't push for the extra rep. The overall health and physical activity of Americans provides a perfect example. Only 5% of the population engages in physical activity on any given day. So, if you're physically active every day of the week, you're doing better than 95% of the country. Yes, it takes commitment, but the action itself isn't that difficult.

Apple (the company) has an edge because it goes the extra mile on design. Google has an edge because it goes the extra mile on providing the fastest and most relevant search results. Companies get the Edge by relentlessly drilling their values into the ethos of every employee. It becomes a pervasive ideology. It's hard to get the Edge to flow through an entire organization. It's naturally much easier on the individual level.

You can (and should) build the Edge into everything you do. Push for the extra rep. Attend one more conference. Take one more class. Focus for one more hour. To truly build the Edge into your life, you need to:

- Seek it out
- Make it a habit
- Enjoy the struggle
- Never settle

Don't worry about being the best.[62] That sets you up for failure and disappointment. It's nearly impossible. Joining the professionally elite, on the other hand, is certainly attainable. You don't need to be the best to succeed. You just need to be better than most.

To boil it all down into a single mantra: avoid complacency. There are no shortcuts and no finish lines. The first nine reps are just as important as the tenth. And when you hit that last rep, you're not finished. You've simply set a new, higher bar to be hurdled later.

---

62   Note: If you're running a business, you *should* worry about being the best. In this context, you need to win the market. There's not much room for second and third when it comes to products and services. But at the individual level (which is what we're discussing here), being #1 isn't mission critical.

Supplements = Awesome

I don't claim to be a nutritional expert, but supplements are awesome. They're often necessary in the world we live in today, especially if you're trying to get the Edge. In the caveman era—the era of hunting and gathering, it was much easier to get our daily fill of vitamins, nutrients, and exercise. Now that we sit in chairs and stare at monitors all day long, it's no wonder our bodies have become deficient.

I don't recommend hooking yourself up to a coffee IV or popping pills all day long, but I don't find fault with giving yourself a physiological nudge every now and then, either. There are plenty of natural ways to improve your energy, awareness, and overall health. I'm not particularly well-versed in this topic, so I won't waste your time with fluff, but you should do your own research and consider adding supplements to your diet. My current regimen is fairly simple:

- I take a daily multivitamin.
- I don't drink coffee, but I'm a huge fan of energy drinks.
- I occasionally take powdered forms of protein, creatine, and glutamine.
- I consume at least one protein shake[63] and one protein bar per day, adding sixty grams of protein and 1,250 calories to my daily diet.[64]

---

63 My protein shake recipe: 16 ounces whole milk, 1 scoop vanilla ice cream, 1 frozen banana, 1 tablespoon peanut butter, 1 tablespoon nutella, 1 teaspoon honey, 3 scoops of Up Your Mass weight gainer or similar product. Blend and serve. Delicious.

64 This is a good thing for me because I struggle to maintain my weight.

While I condone the use of supplements, you should take them with caution. Add only one supplement to your diet at a time. Start with a small dose, increasing incrementally. Periodically remove supplements from your diet as well. If you feel the same or better without them, you probably don't need them. (Remember Dumbo's feather?) Be wary of side effects. I've used supplements for over a decade with no issues, except for the occasional headache. At the first sign of a severe headache, I'll stop taking supplements for a period of one month, introducing them back into my diet, one by one, over several weeks.

Make Health Your Drug

I don't crave pizza, I crave avocados. I don't guzzle alcohol, I guzzle protein shakes. I'm not addicted to TV, I'm addicted to yoga. I don't seek attention, I seek meditation. I don't spend time maintaining an expensive car, I spend time maintaining my priceless body.

It might sound like I'm gloating, but I'm actually telling you how to boost your happiness, productivity, and overall well-being. I don't need to cite a bunch of studies to demonstrate the importance of health. Everyone knows it's important. I've experienced the effects firsthand, and I've also been on both sides.

When I was in my deepest, darkest depression, I was running on empty. I barely weighed 120 pounds. (I'm five foot eleven, so 120 pounds was dangerously skinny). I was getting 3-4 hours of broken sleep per night. My mind was foggy. I was chronically depressed. My diet was almost

---

I'm what's called an "ectomorph."

non-existent. I'd eat only when I was starving, and some-times I'd just let the hunger pass.

Then I committed to P90X, and everything changed. I now exercise every day. I practice yoga, resistance (weight) training, and a host of core and cardiovascular exercises in-cluding kenpo (boxing and kicking), plyometrics (jumping and squatting), and core synergistics (core and multiple-muscle group exercises). I'm now forty pounds heavier, with almost no fat on my body. I sleep more—usually between 7-8 hours a night. I go outside more—usually spending sev-eral hours outdoors on the weekends. I try to do a physical, social activity a few times a month. Examples include hik-ing, paddle-boarding, and beach volleyball.

The result? My happiness has skyrocketed. My pro-ductivity has skyrocketed. My passion has skyrocketed. Meaningful relationships have skyrocketed. Everything is up and to the right. If health isn't your drug—make it your drug. As I've mentioned, there are two fundamental assets in life that unlock the door to everything else. Time is one. Health is the other. Defend both relentlessly. You can thank me later.

My Body Transformation

The above images show my body transformation as a result of P90X. The photos are untouched originals. The picture on the left was taken ninety days prior to the picture on the right. I've included this not to show off my pecs, but to demonstrate the Connection Algorithm in a tangible way. My physical transformation was deliberate. Was it challenging? Yes. Did I have to make sacrifices to do it? Yes. Did I doubt myself throughout the process? Yes. But that's to be expected when living by the Four Cs. Choose, Commit, Create, Connect.

I *chose* to take on the risk of attempting an extreme workout program. I *committed* to it, making it a daily habit. I was able to *create* a meaningful result (please refer to the lovely photos above). Because I did all of these things, I was able to *connect*.

I emailed Beachbody (the company that produces P90X) to share my story. They were impressed, not only with my results, but also with my book. I received a response from Kit Caldicott (Tony Horton's sister), who was kind enough to send the manuscript to Tony. Shortly thereafter, Tony and I spoke on the phone, and he graciously offered to endorse the book, which became a powerful marketing tool. I never expected to chat with the creator of P90X when I first started the program several years earlier, but by following the Four Cs, it happened naturally.

This is the Connection Algorithm in action, my friends. And when you experience it firsthand, it's glorious.

Mind

We've looked at the power of time and how to reclaim it. We've looked at the significance of our physical health as it relates to productivity. Finally, let's consider the impact of our minds.

Our perception and attitude play a huge role in the decisions we make, our ability to solve problems, and ultimately, our capacity for success. Most of the content in this section is common sense, but it will hopefully spark some *"Aha!"* moments, too. Simple truths are often the most elusive, overlooked, and forgotten—so let's dig in and remind ourselves.

The Miracle Wedding

My brother's wedding was the greatest miracle I've ever witnessed. It was simultaneously one of the most terrifying and beautiful experiences of my life, and I'll never forget it. It taught me a valuable lesson about getting things done. Buckle your seatbelts, my friends. This is the story of the Miracle Wedding.

My brother, Ben, and his wife, Rachel, never wanted a traditional wedding. Instead of a tuxedo, Ben wore a slick, gray suit. Instead of a white gown, Rachel wore an earthy, lavender dress. And instead of being married in a church, they planned to be married on a private beach, with their bare feet buried in the sand.

The ceremony was scheduled to take place in Buxton, a tiny beach town on a pencil-thin strip of land just off the coast of North Carolina. The mother of the bride had rented a massive beach house for the reception, which would also double as lodging for the week. For close friends and family, the wedding was meant to be an extended vacation, culminating with the ceremony.

A few days prior to the main event, we received some dreadful news. A nor'easter was forming to the north. For the uninformed, the term *nor'easter* basically means *big-ass storm*. It's a combination of a tropical storm, a hurricane, and a tornado. They happen from time to time in places like Buxton, and that's exactly where this storm was headed. Over the next forty-eight hours, the conditions worsened. Local businesses were told to shut down, and the message from reporters was clear: *Stay indoors.*

On the morning of the wedding, Ben and Rachel were visibly distraught. There were discussions about canceling the ceremony, but it would have been a nightmare to reschedule. This celebration had been nearly a year in the making. The beach house was already paid for, and all the invited guests were en route from across the country. If we canceled, the wedding might *never* happen. We decided to hold firm and hope for the best.

Unfortunately, things only got worse. We learned that the single road into Buxton was completely submerged under water. The state had declared it impassable. Police officers and members of the National Guard were stationed on the mainland to block it off. We needed a Plan B. After a series of nervous blank stares, someone blurted out our next move. "Could we get everyone here via boat?" We all paused initially because it sounded ridiculous, but there wasn't much of a choice. I slammed my credit card down on the table. "This wedding is happening."

With that statement, my mindset changed. Something clicked in my brain. I made a conscious decision that failure was not an option. This mindset must have struck my sister, Nora, at the same time, because we both leapt into action. She was the CEO, and I was the COO. We were t-minus eight hours.

We started calling local marinas and eventually found two captains who were willing to transport our passengers. It wasn't normal protocol, but after some price negotiations, the deal was on. At this point, we had to communicate our plan to over seventy wedding guests. We started making calls, explaining the inherent risk involved. The boats were meant to hold a maximum of twenty-five people, and we were planning to pack over thirty in each—in the middle of a violent storm. We told every guest they could choose to decline, but call after call, the answer was the same: "I'm in."

As I made calls, Nora delegated other tasks. The ceremony now needed to happen indoors instead of outside. We would need designated dressing rooms for guests to change their clothes.[65] All of the food still needed to be prepared. There were a hundred little jobs being done.

---

65 No one could make it to their original lodging. Most everything was shut down.

In the late afternoon, the boats docked. Nora and I drove to the marina to pick up the passengers—and a fleet of nine other vehicles trailed behind us.[66] We didn't realize how bad the conditions were until we got on the road. The standing water had surged to over a foot in some areas, and it splashed onto the hood of our car, flowing over the sideview mirrors as we plowed along. It was surreal, unlike anything I had ever seen. The guests rushed off the boats and into cars as we arrived at the dock. I was frantically directing people like an air traffic controller, the rain hammering down on us in thick, slanted sheets. Grandparents, aunts, uncles, cousins, friends, and even workers from the catering company, were all on this mission together.

By the time we arrived back at the wedding house, the sun had set. The ceremony took place in the guest house, which had been decorated beautifully, almost as if planned that way from the beginning. Nearly seventy guests, all in their most regal attire, watched the bride and groom say their vows as the swampy water rippled in the wind outside.

I gave the best-man speech that night, and my message was simple: Life is hard, life is unexpected, and life is beautiful.[67] There wasn't a dry eye in the house. We had pulled off a miracle, and everyone knew it. Weeks after the wedding, it was reported that the storm had caused over $300 million in damages, and six deaths.[68] Somehow, we didn't let it stop us.

---

66   We had other driver volunteers from the house, and we even enlisted some local taxi services to help pick up the rest of the guests.

67   I had prepared my speech weeks before, and it just so happened that my message was particularly fitting for the wedding itself. The result was an emotional speech, and a room charged with energy.

68   http://tinyurl.com/p45swh7

The most amazing thing about this story is the uncanny speed with which things got done. It was terrifying and stressful, but it worked out. I have no doubt it will remain the most memorable wedding experience of my life.[69] The Miracle Wedding shows us why it's so important to rise up in the face of adversity. Even the most seemingly insurmountable setbacks can be overcome. This story is the best example of Parkinson's Law I've ever witnessed. The storm forced us to get creative and take action. When you're in the middle of a catastrophe, you don't consider the improbability of success. You just get shit done. Curveballs can be a blessing in disguise. Sometimes, they can even spawn miracles.

Think Inside the Box

Almost all constraints come with a built-in silver lining. The Miracle Wedding is a grand example, but there are smaller everyday examples, too. Think about taking a shower, for instance. When you take a shower, you're in a tiny box with some water and soap. There are only so many things you can do with that (I'll spare you the details). Ironically, this frees us. It frees us from looking at our phones. It frees us from checking our email. It frees us from watching TV, from running errands, and from interacting with others. As the hot water washes over us, it's as if we're cleansing our mind's palate, washing all of those external distractions away. This makes the shower a nearly perfect environment for having profound mental breakthroughs.

---

69 Okay, except for my own wedding, if that ever happens. Future wife—I love you.

Even the ultimate confinement—prison—can be freeing. Nelson Mandela spent decades of his life in jail, but many of his most important philosophies, and his sense of leadership, were cultivated behind bars. "It is possible that if I had not gone to jail and been able to read and listen to the stories of many people...I might not have learned these things," Mandela said of the insights he gained during his twenty-seven years in jail. He also understood the value of solitude. He recalls that, "...in jail—especially for those who stayed in single cells—you had enough opportunity to sit down and think."[70]

Storms, showers, and jail cells aren't the only solutions for creating a productive environment. There are plenty of other ways to integrate confinement into your workflow. Limiting your resources, creating self-imposed deadlines, and narrowing your goals are all counterintuitively *positive* constraints. It's not always helpful to think outside the box. Try thinking *inside* the box instead.

Cut the Clutter

A few years back, I discovered a blog called *The Minimalists*.[71] It was created by Joshua Fields Millburn and Ryan Nicodemus. They write about living a meaningful life with less stuff. Their story is very much a proxy for the lifestyle proposed in this book. Joshua and Ryan both had high-paying jobs in corporate America. They had impressively large homes and flashy cars, but they were unfulfilled. At the risk of losing their reputation and clout in the business world, they quit their jobs and started a blog.

---

70   http://tinyurl.com/p7ulumf

71   http://www.theminimalists.com/

The response to their writing has been astounding. Over two million people visited *The Minimalists* blog in 2013, and they've published several books over the past few years, too. They've been featured in numerous media outlets, including CBS, BBC, NPR, USA Today, Forbes, the Wall Street Journal, the Boston Globe, the Chicago Tribune, and the Toronto Star. While their backstory is a perfect example of taking risks, what's most relevant here is their focus on minimalism, and its direct correlation to productivity.

Clutter is the enemy of productivity. Whether mental or physical, it interrupts our focus, distracts us, and weighs us down. This is, as I've explained, why ideas come to us in the shower. In a clutter-free environment, distractions are stripped away, and so we naturally become present and mindful. The minimalistic environment of the shower acts as a productivity enhancer. It stands to reason then, that if we can create a similar environment in *all* areas of our lives, we can exist in a relatively perpetual state of heightened focus, creativity, and clarity.

Reducing clutter requires deliberate action. The common behavior for most people is to acquire more and more stuff over time. We repeatedly buy new clothes, new furniture, and new gadgets—but we rarely get rid of anything. We take classes, join clubs, and make plans with friends—but we rarely say no or cut anything out of our schedule. To declutter your life, you have to change these habits. You have to deliberately clear things away.

When I first started writing this book, my life was jam-packed with *stuff*. My apartment was full of things I didn't need and my schedule barely allowed me to sleep. Over several months, I purged nearly 90% of the clutter from my life.

By refusing to take a new job, I freed up most of my time. I started saying no to most social events. I stopped answering the phone or checking email if I was busy or in the Zone. I cleared out my apartment, selling anything I didn't need.[72]

The emptiness that remained felt unbelievably good. I felt lighter, and my productivity skyrocketed. It's amazing how much you can get done in a clean space with no interruptions. To learn more about decluttering your life, I highly recommend reading Joshua and Ryan's blog (http://www.theminimalists.com/). It will open your eyes to the importance of simplicity.

Attitude Is NOT Everything

Just as the all the *stuff* around you can slow you down, so can the *people* around you. When relationships become strained, attitude matters a lot—but it's not necessarily the cure for every social situation.

I promise you, it's easier to be happy in a spa than a snake pit. Get out of the pit and into the spa. Your problems will go away. Your attitude will naturally improve and people will praise you for being so positive. If you're pissed off all the time, you don't necessarily have an attitude problem. You might just be hanging around too many cold-blooded reptiles.[73] Here's another quote from The Minimalists: "You can't change the people around you, but you can change the

---

72 This isn't an all-or-nothing situation. Don't skip *all* social activities and don't sell *all* of your stuff. Just realize the tendency to over-book and over-consume.

73 If everyone in every situation seems like a snake, you have to start looking inward. But don't do it immediately. Try switching your environment first.

people around you." Take a second to process that one. It's a big factor in avoiding ZombieLand and cultivating a positive, stress-free environment.

I'm Not Smart Enough

A good attitude will help you get through certain roadblocks, but what if you're just not smart enough? What if your mental capacity won't allow you to fulfill your goals?

Paul Graham is the founder of Y Combinator, one of the most successful and sought-after startup accelerators in the tech world. Graham has invested in several blockbuster companies, including AirBNB and Dropbox, both of which are valued in the *billions* at the time of this writing. After investing in hundreds of companies and considering thousands more, Paul Graham has perfected the art of identifying promising startups. His methods may surprise you. In an interview, Graham highlighted two key strategies:

1. Favoring people over product
2. Favoring determination over intelligence

What's most essential for a successful startup?

Graham: The founders. We've learned in the six years of doing Y Combinator to look at the founders—not the business ideas—because the earlier you invest, the more you're investing in the people. When Bill Gates was starting Microsoft, the idea that he had then involved a small-time microcomputer called the Altair. That didn't seem very promising, so you had to see that this 19-year-old kid was going places.

What do you look for?

Graham: Determination. When we started, we thought we were looking for smart people, but it turned out that intelligence was not as important as we expected. If you imagine someone with 100 percent determination and 100 percent intelligence, you can discard a lot of intelligence before they stop succeeding. But if you start discarding determination, you very quickly get an ineffectual and perpetual grad student.[74]

Your intelligence doesn't matter as much as you think it does. If you're reading this book, you're probably more than capable. Your ideas don't matter much, either. What matters most—by far, is your perseverance.

Stop worrying about your mental aptitude. Stop worrying about the viability of the project you're considering. Stop worrying about all the other big decisions keeping you up at night. Instead, focus on relentlessly grinding away at your passion until something incredible happens. Your potential output is governed by your mind*set*, not your mind itself.

Don't Be an Idiot

Now that you're feeling invincible, let me bring you back to reality. When searching for Purpose Arcs and deciding where to place your commitment, don't fool yourself into thinking everything will be a walk in the park. Nothing worthwhile ever is.

---

74   http://tinyurl.com/nabg44z

When I launched my startup, I thought it would be fun and exciting. It was. It was also insanely hard, and I ended up sucking at it pretty badly. Ben Horowitz, famed CEO and venture capitalist, defines the woes of running a company as *The Struggle*: "When you are in the Struggle, nothing is easy and nothing feels right. You have dropped into the abyss and you may never get out."[75]

I don't recommend starting a company unless you have an unending desire to create something valuable, and feel you can endure the most intense psychological stress imaginable, often with zero support, for an extremely long period of time. I'm not telling you to ditch the idea, but it's incredibly difficult. Are you capable of steering the entire ship, or would it be smarter to join a startup that's already found its footing so you can learn the ropes with less pressure? Be sure to ask yourself these tough questions before taking the leap.

You should challenge yourself within the realm of your ability. It might take some experimentation, but you need to aim for the sweet spot, which is outside your comfort zone, and short of the idiot zone. I've messed this up a lot. Nobody likes an idiot, believe me.

---

75   Ben Horowitz, *The Hard Thing About Hard Things.* (Harper Business, 2014).

Be Idiotically Confident

"...over the years, I've made a point of taking chances and gaining confidence in situations that would have scared me earlier."
TONY HORTON

Trinity: Neo, nobody has ever done this before.
Neo: That's why it's going to work.
THE MATRIX

While you have to be realistic, you also have to be confident and willing to test the unknown. If someone insists you can't accomplish something, attempt to prove them wrong before accepting their claim. The desire to push the envelope and risk failure will allow you to settle on a higher plateau. It doesn't mean you'll be able to do what you set out to do, but having the guts to try gives you an edge.

When we see highly successful people, we often assume they have something we don't. They're smarter. They have more money. They have better connections. Sometimes these assumptions are true, but sometimes they aren't. The common thread among successful people is not ability or resources. These things vary. The common thread is risk-taking.

Think about it. For any raging success, there's the possibility of an equally tragic failure. The two outcomes are inherently intertwined. If Facebook crumbles five years from now, it will be an epic failure. That is a risk Mark Zuckerberg lives with every day. He's constantly fighting against it. It's easy to look at success in a vacuum, but it's *always* tied to risk and failure. If you want to increase your chances of great success, you must get comfortable with the uncomfortableness of it. These types of battles aren't won with resources or connections, they're won with your mind.

STEP 4: CONNECT
GROWTH AND RELATIONSHIPS

"I don't know the future. I didn't come here
to tell you how this is going to end. I came here to
tell you how it's going to begin. I'm going to hang
up this phone, and then I'm going to show these
people what you don't want them to see.
I'm going to show them a world without you.
A world without rules and controls, without
borders or boundaries. A world where
anything is possible."

NEO, THE MATRIX

Congratulations, you've made it to the final step! This is the easy part. Choosing, Committing, and Creating is a long grind, but Connecting is often effortless. This section defines the Connection Algorithm (the actual formula), demonstrates the entire process in action, gives practical, real-world examples of how to connect, and teaches you how to give back after finding success. It describes the boundless world of opportunity in front of you—the world that exists outside of ZombieLand.

The Connection Algorithm Defined

Drumroll please. It's time to unveil the algorithm. According to my trusty friend Wikipedia, an *algorithm* is:

> ...an effective method expressed as a finite list of well-defined instructions for calculating a function.

Starting from an initial state and initial input (perhaps empty), the instructions describe a computation that, when executed, proceeds through a finite number of well-defined successive states, eventually producing an "output" and terminating at a final ending state.

Wow, it doesn't get much drier than that. To translate: An algorithm is a series of steps. For the purposes of this book, I've used the term loosely. While the Connection Algorithm doesn't present a *specific* series of steps to follow, it does define broad behavioral steps, which are meant to be repeated in a continuous loop.

You may be wondering why the algorithm hasn't been presented until now. The answer is that it *has* been presented. You already know the algorithm. The challenge is not understanding it. The challenge is being brave enough to execute it. The Connection Algorithm is the Four Cs:

1. Choose
2. Commit
3. Create
4. Connect

The cycle should repeat throughout your life. *Risk-taking* is the driver behind every step. The entire process is about being bold and taking chances. Because risk-taking is so critical, I've created a second formula that serves as an equally important framework. It presents the Connection Algorithm as a function of risks and relationships:

$$f(pg) = (ri)(x) + (re)(y)$$

Where:
pg = Personal Growth
ri = Risks
x = A numeric variable
re = Relationships
y = A numeric variable

So, in its simplest form, this formula states that your personal growth is proportional to the number of risks you take plus the number of relationships you build. I considered an equation that accounted for other variables like time, relevancy, intensity, and diminishing returns, but it made the formula unnecessarily complicated. So instead, I've qualified each variable further in the sections below. These sections will help you understand the formula's nuances and real-world applications.

Personal Growth (pg)

This term encompasses various characteristics, including intellect, confidence, clout, and reputation. The list of ingredients will differ per individual. It's important to determine what constitutes personal growth for *you,* specifically, and to know what you want to do with that growth. After you've defined growth in the context of *you,* the goal is to increase your capability in those areas. There is no end to this goal. It's a perpetual quest.

Because personal growth isn't quantifiable, it can only be measured in terms of relativity. Your aim is to be able to look back at any point in time and know you've grown since then. Be diligent in finding appropriate measuring sticks. For example, getting a promotion at work may not be a legitimate measure of growth. Sometimes, titles are empty labels, representing nothing more than tenure. Likewise, if you're learning skills that aren't related to your interests, that's not the best kind of growth.

Don't feel pressure to make great leaps and bounds consistently. There will be periods in which you grow tremendously quickly, and periods in which you grow slowly. Your growth curve will also flatten out over time. This is natural. We learn more—at a faster rate—when we're younger. All of these things are okay. The only situation you want to avoid is prolonged stagnation—zero growth. To put this in the context of the formula—when your growth is flatlining, you should take new risks or build new relationships, or both. Remember that every new risk and relationship should be fueled by *passion*. (Recall the Happiness Pyramid).

Risk (ri)

There are different types of risk. We could slice it up a million different ways, but let's separate it into two categories: *Shallow Risks* and *Deep Risks*. Shallow Risks are risks with minimal downside. An example would be approaching someone you find attractive and striking up a conversation. Worst case scenario: the person dislikes you and you move on. Best case: you just found the love of your life. Deep Risks are risks with a potentially big downside. An example would be quitting your high-paying job to build a startup. Best case scenario: you become a wildly successful entrepreneur. Worst case: you slowly fail, losing money, friendships, sanity, and years of your life in the process.

You should take Shallow Risks often. You have nothing to lose, and everything to gain. You should also take Deep Risks—when you can live with the worst case scenario.[76] To quell the fear, mitigate risk whenever possible.[77] If you're planning to quit your job, save up some money first, and ask your friends if you could sleep on their couch for six months if things don't go as planned. It's nice to know you have support if everything falls apart. Build that into your decision-making process, realizing you don't need much to survive. (Remember the MVP discussion? 30K should get you launched and in a position to raise additional funds.) Taking risks doesn't mean being a daredevil, or skydiving without a parachute. It means pushing your limits, trying new things, and making calculated, bold decisions.

Andy Dunn, the founder and CEO of Bonobos, wrote an amazing article about the risk of *not* taking risks. He argues that the biggest risk is the risk not taken. If you haven't read the article, you should,[78] but here's my favorite part, where Andy brilliantly explains why the secret to living without regrets is to take every risk you ever consider:

Very little is obvious in the research on human decision-making and happiness. Very few things are

---

76   Deep Risks often have big rewards, even if you fail. This is why they're worth it.

77   Don't use the absence of a safety net as an excuse for not starting. A lot of people do this. It's a cop out.

78   https://medium.com/i-m-h-o/40cf0a8919cb

proven. One thing that is proven is this: the only re-grets octogenarians have are for the risks not taken.

Here's why: If the risk taken does pan out, it is good. But if it doesn't—and here's the key thing—we find a way to justify the risk taken as learning.

Learning is not an empty justification. This is a cliché—but learning is what life is all about. If we look at this backwards, we see that personal growth comes from learning, and learning comes from risk-taking, which is exactly why risk-taking is core to the Connection Algorithm.

Relationships (re)

In the context of the formula, a *relationship* is an authentic, two-way connection between you and a Connector. For a relationship to be meaningful, you have to genuinely care about the other person, and they have to genuinely care about you. The relationship is not a means to an end, but an end in itself. This doesn't mean you can't get help from a Connector before you have a relationship with them. You have to start somewhere. Often times, relationships form out of an initial favor.

Relationships are critical because they can present new opportunities, while simultaneously providing a support system to help you overcome adversity and bounce back from risks that result in failure. Although the formula implies that having many relationships is better than having only a few, this is untrue, because it's impossible to maintain an infinite number of *authentic* relationships. There is also a threshold where the effect of adding additional relation-ships—even authentic ones—becomes negligible in relation to personal growth. This is discussed further in the following section.

Graphs and Stuff

Remember, the formula is simplified. Let's dig a little deeper and consider the elements that were left out. This stuff is important.

The first step is actually a leap. The first big risk you take is the most impactful. Subsequent risks are still meaningful, but have diminishing returns.

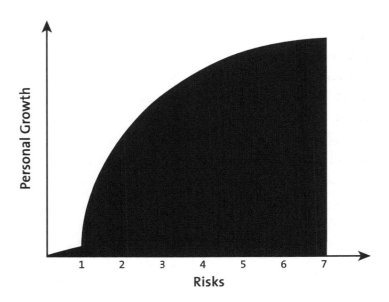

The same holds true for relationships.

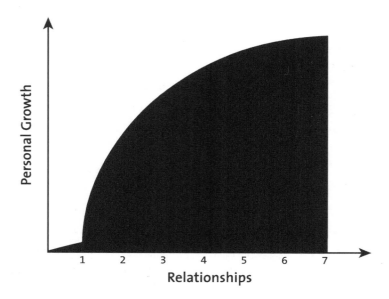

To understand why this is the case, let's consider a hypothetical example. Suppose you're the owner of a small business, and a prominent media outlet runs a positive story about your company's progress. The coverage could affect your company dramatically. It could be the spark that allows you to raise your next round of funding, or close the partner deal you've been working on, or hire the key employee you've been chasing after.

Now, consider if the company was featured by *two* publications instead of one. Would it change anything? It would certainly help, but getting a single outlet to run the story is much more important than getting a second, or a third, or a fourth. The bulk of the results come from the initial breakthrough. The rest is gravy.[79] This is why *starting* is so important.

---

79   This is the 80/20 rule in action, yet again.

Each step is unique. The impact of each risk and relationship will vary. If you take a small risk that doesn't map directly to your definition of personal growth, that risk will have a low impact. In contrast, if you cultivate a relationship with the most powerful person in your industry, your growth will skyrocket. So, your growth trajectory won't necessarily be as smooth as the above graphs suggest. It will follow the same general curve, but it might include some irregular spikes and slower growth periods as well.

Consider an example in the film industry. Let's imagine you're an aspiring actor or actress. Naturally, you want to meet Connectors in your field of study. While auditioning for a low level role in a big film, you happen to meet one of the best agents in the business. He is undoubtedly a Connector. You cultivate a strong relationship with the agent and he becomes your first true conduit to accelerated growth. A few months later, the agent introduces you to Martin Scorsese, one of the most successful and influential directors in cinematic history. Good news—Scorsese loves you and quickly becomes your friend. You now have a relationship with an A-List Connector.

In this example, the bond with Scorsese is far more impactful than the bond with the agent, even though Scorsese is not the initial connection. Here's the graph of your personal development in this case:

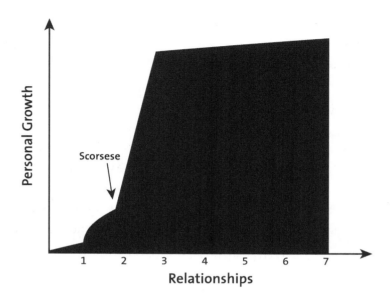

The first connection with the agent gives you a nice lift. But the second connection—Scorsese, rockets you nearly to the top. Anyone after that still gives you an increase, but it's negligible. Moral of the story: The specific risks and relationships you choose matter a lot. You don't have unlimited time, so find the very best ones and act on them as quickly as possible.

Depth matters. The depth of your risks and relationships matter, too. In the previous example, if your connection with Scorsese never develops beyond the first hello, the graph never shoots skyward. On the risk side of the equation, common factors are time and persistence. If you don't put the time and effort into the risk, the resulting benefits will be reduced, or eliminated completely. Depth and quality, over quantity, is always the best approach.

Time matters. Time isn't included in the formula, but it's a critical part of the real-world equation. The point of this is to accelerate your growth. You have a finite amount of time on this planet, so the goal is to advance as quickly as possible. To maximize the acceleration:

1. Start now. Act on the Four Cs and the formula *today*. If you have kids, let them in on the secret, too. The earlier they start, the better.
2. Go straight to the top. Take risks and build relationships that map *directly* to your personal growth. Again, quality over quantity. Aim high.

The Path to Being Connected

The most influential Connectors in my life are David Cohen and Brad Feld. They're both A-List investors in the startup world. They're the equivalent of Tom Hanks and Denzel Washington if we were still talking about the movie business. As you can imagine, these guys are extremely hard to reach without a personal intro, or a killer product.

I'm fortunate because I can count on David and Brad for support, advice, and encouragement, whenever I need it. We've exchanged hundreds of emails, had countless phone conversations, hung out together, enjoyed meals together, and partied together. I consider these guys—these brilliant, blue-chip investors—as friends. These types of relationships don't just fall into your lap. So how did I do it? Was it by chance? Dumb luck? Maybe. But what if it was something else? What if it was more than that? To answer this question, we need to take a trip down memory lane.

I grew up in a small town in Maryland. I participated in a lot of extracurricular activities throughout high school—from wrestling, to choir, to lacrosse. Like most kids, I had no idea what I wanted to do when I grew up. I was just having fun. When it was time to graduate, I took the next logical step and went to college—but I didn't go to the state school like most of my friends. I wanted to expand my horizons and try something new. Choosing a university was difficult. There were a lot of elements to consider. I knew I wanted a big school with strong athletics and great academics, but I wasn't sure about location. My parents hadn't urged me to stay close to home, but they hadn't urged me to move far away either. The decision was entirely up to me.

I researched over 100 different colleges, settling on about ten that I wanted to visit. Duke University, the University of Virginia, and the University of Michigan, were among my favorites. Something about my visit to Michigan captivated me. The air was crisp, I liked the campus, the people were nice, and the architecture was beautiful. It just felt right. Michigan was also coincidentally the furthest away from home, but that didn't stop me from applying. It was my number one choice, and I got in.

Enrolling at Michigan was the first bold decision of my life. It turned out to be one of the best decisions I've ever made, but it didn't seem that way at the time. When my father drove away after helping me move in, I was scared shitless. I was 500 miles away from everything I had ever known.

The entire first year was tough. Although there were plenty of positive things going on, I was painfully homesick. I considered transferring to my state school, the University of Maryland, between my freshman and sophomore years, but eventually resolved to give Michigan another try. And over the next three years, I had the time of my life. I made new friends, joined a fraternity, sang in an a cappella group, traveled to Acapulco and Toronto, became enamored with Michigan football, and so much more. When it was all over, I realized the benefits of working through my fears. I learned that taking risks is terrifying, but necessary in leaping forward.

At the start of my senior year, I was on track to earn my degree in architecture. After the second day of class, I found myself sitting in the studio late at night, cutting pieces of cardboard. I was layering the pieces on top of each other, one by one, to form a three dimensional model. As I worked, a nervous voice in my head kept asking, *"Is this really what you want to do?"* Architecture was a difficult discipline. To get my masters degree, I would need another two years of graduate study. I loved architecture in general, but I didn't love the day-to-day grind of my coursework, or the prospect of doing that type of work after graduation.

For some reason, I found myself constantly thinking about business ideas, startups, and the possibility of forming my own company one day. I couldn't escape it. The urge was so strong that I sat in on some business courses over the next few days, and I was immediately hooked. A few days after that, I quit the architecture program. I remember crying that night. I was scared shitless—again.

It was too late for me to enter the business program and graduate on time, and I couldn't afford to attend college for more than four years. Michigan was ridiculously expensive for out-of-state students, so my loans were already astronomical. I searched through all the degrees offered at Michigan and found one in the sociology program called *Sociology with sub-concentrations in Business, Economics, and Society.*

Several intro-level business courses were included in the program. I could also graduate on time if I packed my schedule with the necessary classes. Perfect! By the third week of school, I was caught up on my coursework and on my way to earning a quasi business-related degree. While I wasn't officially enrolled in the business school, the intro-level business courses gave me a broad understanding of things like marketing—and all of the sociology courses were still geared toward business or economics in some way. I also sat in on higher level business courses whenever I could.

Later in my senior year, I started interviewing with consulting firms. Even though I wasn't a member of the business school, I attended all of the recruitment events, so the recruiters just assumed I was in the program. I scored interviews with most of the top firms. I was flown out to New York City and Chicago to meet with executives, and put up in ritzy hotels with the rest of the candidates. Although none of the firms offered me a position, I learned a valuable lesson: I was able to break through boundaries, simply by testing them. The main obstacle was my mind.

Getting rejected by the management companies did create a problem though. It left me without a job at graduation.

I was scared shitless once again. Naturally, I decided to take another risk. Instead of moving back home, I moved to New York City, knowing Manhattan would offer more compelling job opportunities than suburban Maryland. (I should also mention that I was dating a girl who lived on the upper east side at the time. I have to admit—that played a role in my decision too.)

Three months later, I was living in my girlfriend's mother's apartment, still searching frantically for a job. I was blasting my resume out to every company I could find, but it didn't seem to matter. Getting desperate, I began applying to restaurant jobs, and eventually found an opening at an upscale seafood place.

A week later, I received a phonecall from a guy named Wiley. He was the VP of SeamlessWeb, a startup that operated an online food ordering service. At the time, this was a new concept. The company was relatively small—about fifty people, but it was growing like crazy. Wiley had a low, scratchy voice and an infectious energy. He talked fast. He convinced me to come in for an interview and I met him in person later that week. I loved everything about him and the company, but unfortunately, he didn't hire me. He said everyone liked me, but they didn't need me. They were hiring a bunch of interns for much cheaper than they'd have to pay a full-time employee. Over the next few weeks, I emailed Wiley incessantly, begging him to hire me anyway. To my surprise, he eventually obliged. All of my risky decisions and persistence had *finally* paid off. I was working at a hot startup in New York City. It was my first taste of success.

I worked at SeamlessWeb for about six months, at which point another recruiter came knocking on my door. I guess the job market was heating up again.[80] The recruiter worked for Keynote Systems, a publicly traded tech consulting company that had been extremely popular before the dotcom bubble burst. The stock traded at $154 at its peak in early 2000 before plummeting to $14 in 2001. The stock price never recovered, but they stayed in business, and I came onboard in 2005. I got a considerable pay raise, which was the main impetus for taking the job—but I was also hoping to gain some insight on website usability, and learn how tech companies were operated. I thought it could help me run my own startup someday.

Keynote never prepared me to run a startup, but it introduced me to someone who could. In the summer of 2006, an undergraduate student from the Wharton School came into our office to interview for a summer internship. His name was Joe. As we went through our interview questions, Joe leaned back in his chair and casually gave us the answers, as if he was reciting the alphabet. He was surprisingly calm, confident, and sharp throughout the entire meeting. It was clear that he didn't need the position. He was completely overqualified.

---

80   SeamlessWeb was acquired by Aramark soon after I left. Several years later, SeamlessWeb merged with GrubHub Inc., which IPO'd in 2014 with a market cap of nearly $3 billion. Although I came into the company six years after its founding in 1999, it was still very much a startup when I joined. I didn't have equity in the company, but I was fortunate to experience the early stages of a startup that would eventually find great success. This was mostly blind luck, but I sensed the company was onto something from the moment I met the team. Wiley later went on to found a company called Single Platform, which sold to Constant Contact for $100 million in 2012.

Despite his overqualification, Joe took the job anyway, and we became friends. About a year later, he would become my cofounder. Joe is the smartest person I've ever met. I only met him because I happened to be working at Keynote, and because he happened to accept the internship position that summer. The chemistry between us was strong. It seemed we were destined to go into business together.

In April of 2007, Joe and I submitted a business idea to a new startup accelerator called TechStars. When the TechStars founder and CEO, David Cohen, contacted us and told us we had been selected to join the inaugural summer session in Boulder, Colorado, there wasn't any hesitation in my mind. I quit my job the very next day. It was time to pack my bags and head to the mountains—which brings us back full circle.

I didn't meet David and Brad by chance. I met them because I went to the University of Michigan instead of my state school, because I decided against transferring, because I switched my field of study at the 11th hour, because I moved to New York City without a job after graduation, because I insisted on landing a position at SeamlessWeb even after being denied, because I hopped jobs in search of building my own startup, because I met Joe, and because we applied to TechStars—which was completely new and unproven at the time.

It might sound like I'm preaching about fate, but I'm not. This wasn't destined to be. Rather, it was the result of a string of incredibly risky decisions. *My decisions* led me to meet amazing people. It wasn't by chance at all.

Get In Early

One of the best ways to connect is to get in early. My startup joined TechStars in 2007, which was their first year of operation. TechStars was totally different back then. There was only one program in Boulder, Colorado, and the pool of applicants was relatively small. Even in that forgiving environment, I'm pretty sure our company was the last one picked. We hardly had a demo—much less a prototype—and our initial idea was a dud. Thankfully, we still made the cut.

Once admitted, we received a lot of attention from the mentors and directors, which helped us tremendously. I'm sure the TechStars advisors are still top-notch today, but they took extra care to build relationships with the founders in that critical first year. TechStars knew that much of its success would hinge on the strength of its network and reputation. By joining the program in its inaugural year, we received special treatment.

When my startup first launched, we built products for the Facebook Platform. The platform had just opened—it was a new frontier and we took advantage of it. Because the platform was so new, Facebook users were excited to try new apps and click on ads. We were able to amass a huge user base and earn considerable advertising income in those early days, simply because the platform was fresh. Years later, it became much harder to thrive on the Facebook Platform because the market had matured and there was more competition. Users also became less interested in the platform in general, because the novelty of using third party applications had worn off.

Even though the market eventually shifted to mobile platforms, we were able to take advantage of Facebook's offering by getting in early, and it served as the launchpad for our company. The same is true for a handful of other notable companies, like Zynga and Zoosk. They both relied heavily on the Facebook platform when it first launched, and they've both grown into billion dollar businesses.

Much of my success has come from getting in early. Is it risky? Yes. Potentially life-changing? Yes. Just the way I like it.

Meng To's Master Plan

Getting in early with an institution like TechStars is useful, but not mandatory. This is especially the case when serving an emerging market, because it often affords immediate growth. If you can serve the market early, you might not need outside help.

If you recall, back in Section 3 (Create), our Cambodian friend Meng To was creating a digital book called *Design+Code,* using the experience and knowledge he had gained from nearly fifteen years of side projects, freelancing, odd jobs, and failed businesses. He had been through three of the Four Cs: Choose, Commit, Create—and finally all of his struggles were paying off. Meng had discovered a need in the market at the intersection of design and programming. He was capitalizing on a trend, spearheaded by Sketch. The demand, paired with the audience Meng had built online, meant immediate sales. After the book's initial release, he quickly found financial freedom, which allowed him to pursue his passions even further.

Meng is now focusing on *Design+Code* full time. It's all he does. His next step, naturally, is to connect with the community he created. He's expanding his operations, teaching Sketch courses in person throughout various cities across the globe.[81]

Meng offered some great—albeit familiar—advice during our discussions. It's the same advice you'll hear from every Connector you ever meet, but it's worth repeating. He says, "You will always be nagged about your decisions and there will always be second guesses about your decisions. The first time I wrote about Sketch, there were a ton of people saying, *'Who is this guy? And why is he talking about Sketch? What is this new application?'* Or, with writing a book, people would say, *'You're not even a writer. You don't even write amazing English!'* I think the only sensible response to these types of [statements] is: *'So what?'*" Meng pauses, then repeats it again: "So what?"

"People also make things out to be more visionary than they actually are. The truth is, at the moment you're making the decisions, it's not that clear exactly what you're going to do. Now that I've done it, of course it makes sense. But back then, I just had a general idea that I wanted to help designers learn things that I think are important, and I

---

81   Remember that year of traveling that Meng spent with his girlfriend? Well, it's now paying dividends. Meng is a very experienced and savvy traveler, which helps him efficiently get from city to city as he teaches Sketch classes all over the world. This is an example of Connecting the Dots Later. Trust that your experiences will serve a purpose in the future, no matter how unclear it seems at the time.

wanted to do that in the best way that I could. That's all I thought about. I didn't think about teaching, I didn't think about traveling full-time like I am, I didn't even think about writing a book before I wrote it. Sure, it makes sense, when you write a dozen articles, for that to eventually grow into a book. But at the time of all the decisions, you're so driven that you're just *working*."

"You have a figment of a plan. You don't have an exact plan of how it's going to be executed. You have a loose idea, like, *'I know I'm going to travel for a few months. I know that I'm going to meet with this person. I know that this is the topic I want to write about. I know that these are the problems I want to solve. And I know that I want to package it in a way that I'm good at.'* Of course you know all of these little things. You just don't know how all of them are going to come together and what exactly it's going to look like."

When I interviewed Meng, he was in Milan (to teach a Sketch class, of course) and I was in Los Angeles—but I could see his facial expressions clearly through my computer screen. He looked wise. He looked like someone who had figured things out. The poor Cambodian immigrant boy was now a happy, wealthy man. He had found his Purpose Arc and followed the Four Cs: Choose, Commit, Create, Connect. Meng somehow inherently knew the formula, and now he's traveling the world, living his dream.

Don't Ask for Help

Most scenarios are not like Meng's story. It's hard to be a one-man-band. If you need additional resources and expertise to accomplish your goals, that's perfectly fine—but you need to do it the right way.

So, let me drill this into your skull a little further: The purpose of a connection is not to get help. The purpose of a connection is to build a relationship. When a relationship is built, it's no longer just an avenue for help—it's two friends supporting each other. The true value is in the relationship, not one-off favors. This means you should build connections early, *before* you need help. You should find the common ground that brings you and the other person together. Connect on that level first. It's best if the initial connection happens offline, although it's possible for relationships to develop in the digital world, too. Matt Galligan, CEO of Circa and fellow TechStars alum, describes making connections in the context of dating:

> If your goal is a career, and your goal is developing a network, you need to understand that it's exactly like dating. Your goal at the end of the day should be to get another date, not just hook up.[82]

Ask for Help

Not all help is created equal. Asking a highly connected person for big favors without any intention of forming a relationship is a horribly bad idea—but asking for minor support is a great one.

---

82   http://tinyurl.com/qaam9pg

When I see a homeless person, I think to myself, "*Gosh, that must be tough.*" I'm sure it is in fact tough, but homeless people who beg for money do so because it actually works on some level. I'd be curious to know how much money the best performing homeless people make per year, versus the lousiest performers. I bet the disparity is substantial. There are plenty of variables that could contribute to a homeless person's effectiveness, but the most critical is likely traffic density (i.e. location).

Essentially, it's a numbers game. Some people give money to the poor, and some don't. There's a higher probability of getting a donation if I ask ten people versus five people. If I ask 100 people, there's an even better chance. And if I ask 1,000, I'm probably rolling in dough. Okay, maybe I'm not rolling in dough, but you get the idea. If you ask enough people for something reasonable, even for nothing in return, you'll probably get it—eventually. The homeless guy in Times Square is most certainly doing better than the homeless guy on Main Street in Bumblefuck, USA.

Notice that homeless people don't demand a minimum donation either. They accept and appreciate anything. This flexible mentality can (and should) be used in your own life, too. A CEO isn't going to give you two hours of his time for nothing in return. But he might give you two minutes. If he doesn't, ask again. If he still refuses, ask a few more times. Then ask a different CEO. And another. Then ask for one minute instead of two. You get the idea. Eventually, with enough attempts and tweaking, someone will help you out.

Cold Calling

Cold calling works more often than you would think. If you're doing something meaningful, people can be surprisingly receptive. When I was figuring out what to do after leaving my startup, I had two main focuses. One focus was this book. The other was a mobile app. I experimented with both ideas for a few months.

After several weeks, I had a prototype of the app I was considering. The prototype was a set of high-fidelity mockups designed in PhotoShop.[83] I imported the mockups into a program called InVision. The software allowed me to link the designs together so it felt like a working product, even though it was nothing more than artwork. I then created a demo video of the product using Vimeo, a free video sharing site. Finally, I reached out for some feedback.

The feedback was mixed, which ultimately led me to focus on the book, but presenting the prototype was an interesting experience. All of the development firms I contacted responded back. This was somewhat expected because I was a potential customer. Still, I was surprised to get responses from *all* of them. It validated my work. All of my advisors also responded. This was expected, too, since I already knew them.

The most surprising response came from Naveen Selvadurai, one of the cofounders of a company called Four-Square. I had never spoken to Naveen before. I didn't know

---

83   I learned how to create wireframes and mockups while at my company, and it turns out to be a very useful skill. This is an example of a byproduct, and Connecting the Dots Later.

him. I just knew he was talented. From what I could glean, he was very down-to-earth, likeable, and bright. I found Naveen on Facebook and sent him a message. The message was very simple. I said hello, told him what I was working on, and sent him the demo video. He responded a few days later and we had a conversation about the product. He even gave me some useful insights.

I didn't expect to hear from Naveen. His interest and kindness blew me away. Don't assume people are unreachable, even if you've never spoken to them before—even if they're founders, or CEOs, or millionaires.[84]

Roll Down the Hill

Snowball sampling[85] is a research methodology often used in sociological and statistical studies. It's a very simple concept. The researcher will identify her target sample and then reach out to people within that community, often offering an incentive to participate in the study. After making a connection with someone, the researcher will ask that person to reach out to another personal contact who also fits the requirements of the target sample. Participants are acquired this way throughout the study, similar to how a snowball picks up additional snow as it rolls down a hill. The technique is also known as *chain sampling* or *referral sampling*.

---

84   Of the people I contacted, there were also a handful who never responded. Don't assume everyone will respond either. It's nothing personal.

85   http://en.wikipedia.org/wiki/Snowball_sampling

I used this method in college to interview Pfizer employees for a case study that would eventually become my honors thesis.

Snowball sampling is often used for studies that involve hidden or elusive communities, such as drug dealers or pornstars. Because these people are hard to reach, tapping into the community through personal connection lines is more effective than reaching out to everyone individually. If you want to link up with a bunch of drug dealers and pornstars, you now have the formula. But this sampling technique isn't just useful for undercover communities. It's a great formula for meeting *anyone* who would normally be difficult to reach.

The most important step in this process is the initial connection. You don't necessarily need to meet the head honcho, you just need to get plugged into the community and start working your way through connection lines. Even if you never meet the head honcho, you'll meet all kinds of other amazing people in the process. Remember that an incentive is usually beneficial in making the initial connection.

When applying to TechStars, my cofounder and I were essentially offering an incentive to get access to a community. We described ourselves, presented our idea, and explained how it could become a thriving business. Tech-Stars reviewed our pitch and decided it was worth their time. They believed they could potentially get something in return, so they plugged us into their network.

From that point forward, I was introduced to countless venture capitalists, CEO's, and startup gurus who would have otherwise been nearly impossible to reach. I was snowball sampling without realizing it. Instead of building a sample for a research study, though—I was building personal relationships. I was connecting with awesome people who could bring significant meaning to my life. Don't think of it as networking. Think of it as finding useful communities. Plug yourself into these communities and start exploring. Start rolling down the hill.

Where to Connect

Connecting has everything to do with where you put yourself. Do you live in a rural town, or a city? Are you engaging in activities outside of your job, or just watching TV and sleeping? Are you going to events where other smart people are likely to be hanging out, or are you going to the bar? Are you constantly socializing with your slacker friends, or your ambitious friends? These choices greatly influence who you will meet, and who you will become. Here are some of the best places to meet amazing people:

Extracurriculars

If you're following your passions, you should be doing it both independently *and* socially. Is there a club you could join that relates to your interests? If not, could you start one? This can be done in the physical world or the digital world. Start a group on LinkedIn. Build a following by writing articles on Medium.[86] Plan a Meetup. There are plenty of options for taking your interests to the social arena. When

---

86 Meng To used this approach with great success.

you reach out to the community to demonstrate your passions, you'll naturally attract others who share those same passions. People don't join clubs and groups because they're mildly interested, they join because they're *deeply* interested. These are the people you want to meet.

- LinkedIn: https://www.linkedin.com/
- Medium: https://medium.com/
- Meetup: http://www.meetup.com/

Internships

My cofounder and I met because he decided to do an internship at the company that previously employed me. Being an intern can do amazing things for your career and your life. The concept of an internship is similar to the concept of an accelerator program, in that the primary focus is not the financial gain. The primary focus is the experience, the connections, and the mentorship you will receive. If you do an internship, be sure to go into it with this mentality. Befriend the most impressive employees. Soak everything in. The money will last a few months, but the connections and experiences will last a lifetime.

College

College is one of the best breeding grounds to find and build relationships with Connectors (or future Connectors). College campuses are filled with awesome people. The professors, students, and grad students have all been prescreened for you by the admissions office and the hiring department. Schedules are also more flexible in college, so it's easier to work on group projects. The benefit you get from going to class is secondary, in my opinion, to the benefit you can get from connecting with brilliant people and cultivating long-lasting friendships. I'm not saying you should skip class completely, but take advantage of the community around you. If you only go to college for your degree, you're missing out.

Accelerators

Startup accelerators, like TechStars, are a new kind of university. I highly recommend them as an alternative or supplemental education to college. Accelerators are extremely competitive and focused. They naturally facilitate a tightly-knit community that's collaborative and supportive. It's like college on crack.

My experience with TechStars has been nothing short of amazing. Seven years after graduating from the program, I'm still in contact with mentors and friends whom I met there. The resources and camaraderie within the network are unlike anything else I've ever experienced. Through email and other TechStars-specific communication tools, I've witnessed CEO's connecting with each other, exclusive partnerships with leading companies like Google and Facebook, and special deals and perks that only TechStars can offer.

Joining an accelerator program can change your life. The title of *accelerator* is appropriate. It connects you with brilliant people, which then speeds up your professional *and* personal development. You don't necessarily need to apply to an accelerator program as a company. You can also apply as an employee or an intern. Getting yourself into the ecosystem is valuable, from any angle.

Startups

Startups are inherently filled with Connectors. These are self-starters and risk takers. When you launch or work at a startup, you're joining a club of people who are just as crazy and hopeful as you are.

While a startup can be an endpoint, it can also create new opportunities for the future. Paypal's original core team is commonly referred to as the Paypal Mafia because most of the early employees launched other companies after Paypal was bought by eBay. Here are some of the most well-known Paypal Mafia members: Peter Thiel (early investor in Facebook, founder of Palantir, managing partner of Founders Fund), Reid Hoffman (founder of LinkedIn), Max Levchin (founder of Slide), Roelof Botha (partner at Sequoia Capital), David Sacks (founder of both Geni and Yammer), Chad Hurley (founder of YouTube), Elon Musk (founder of both SpaceX and Tesla Motors), Jerry Stoppleman (founder of Yelp), and Dave McClure (founder of 500 Startups). Is it a coincidence that so many of Paypal's early team members went on to do amazing things? I don't think so. They all knew what they were getting into when they started their follow-up ventures. They had already been through it at PayPal.

Online Forums/Blogs/Apps

There's a rich community of thinkers who hang out in the commenting layer of the internet. Blogging platforms and communication apps offer similar environments. It's easy to find people with common interests through these channels because they're usually topic-specific, and searchable.

When considering new projects to work on after I left my company, I came across a new location-based chatting app called Ripple. The app was built by a scrappy startup—a team of three guys. I got in touch with the founder relatively easily, and he kindly explained that he was busy working on Ripple and didn't have time to entertain other projects. His response was completely understandable.

But then, after doing some research online, I discovered his life mirrored the principles of the Connection Algorithm perfectly. In addition to building Ripple, he was in the process of writing a book about a new software program called Sketch. His name? Meng To. I asked Meng if he'd be willing to share his story with me, and of course, he agreed.

The simple act of downloading a chatting app led me to meet a fellow Connector who then became an integral part of this book. The world is full of these opportunities. I wasn't necessarily looking for a connection. I just had my eyes open.

Commenting Systems

Integrated commenting systems like Disqus, or standalone commenting services like Quora, are also fantastic places to make connections. There are a ton of smart people commenting on the internet because it builds their credibility. Digging around for a few hours can lead to top-tier Connectors. When you find someone of interest, bookmark his information. Send him a message after you've completed Step 3 (Create).

Meetups

Meetups can be a great place to—you guessed it—meet people. I attended a few Meetups several years ago through www.meetup.com for the purpose of recruiting local talent for my startup. If you attend a Meetup, you have to be outgoing. If you're not willing to talk to strangers, don't go. It'll be a waste of your time. Meetups can be awkward because people are often purposefully networking at them, which I find off-putting. I prefer environments where people aren't expecting to be bombarded with business cards. That said, Meetups allow you to connect with a targeted group of people in a short period of time.

Conferences

Conferences are like meetups on steroids. I've been to very few, but I plan on attending more, and you should, too. Valuable connections can be made at conferences if you're at the right place, at the right time, with the right value proposition. Some of the biggest conferences I know of are SXSW (South by Southwest), 99U, TechCrunch Disrupt, and Launch Festival. These are mostly tech and design-focused conferences, but there are conferences for everything. Do a simple Google search to find conferences specific to your area of interest. Go to at least one. I'm planning on taking my own advice, so maybe I'll see you there.

Hanging Out

Last but not least, you can meet amazing people by simply hanging out. That's right—you just have to be hanging out with the right crowd. This past weekend, I played beach volleyball. Then I went to a bar. I met entrepreneurs in both locations. One of the guys I met was operating a real estate company in Australia, but looking to start something new in the United States. His friends run their own beer company. Everyone in the group was very entrepreneurial. I met these people because I was originally invited by my college friend, Simon, who lives nearby. He graduated from Michigan's business school and works in technology sales. He knows everyone. Smart people know other smart people, so go hang out with them and see what happens.

Personal Values and Habits

While at my startup, one of my responsibilities was to distill our company values into a concise, functional document. It was meant to define our company and everyone in it. It was basically our constitution.

Most companies have a similar document, or set of documents. They go by various names—*Core Values, Cultural Habits, The Company Handbook*, etc. The purpose of these documents is to define the company's cultural and operational beliefs. This is helpful because it directs behavior, aids in decision-making, and keeps everyone focused on a shared vision. After establishing the company values, I realized they could also be considered *personal* values, even though our intention had only been to apply them to our organization.

As individuals, we rarely think of values in such a formal way. It makes sense for an organization to create unifying cultural documents so the values of that organization can be disseminated across the team. As individuals though, shouldn't we just inherently *know* what we stand for? When

I asked myself this question, I realized—to my surprise—that I didn't really know my values. I had a broad sense, but it wasn't crystal clear. So I wrote them down, taking a *lot* of cues from our company documents. Here they are:

Values
1. I am my own **leader**
2. I am **passionate** in my endeavors
3. I value **quality**
4. I am **explorative**
5. I am **innovative**
6. I am **honest**
7. I am **caring**
8. I am **respectful**
9. I am **confident**, but humble
10. I stay **grounded**

Our company also created a habits list. Here's mine, again adapted from the company's version:

Habits
1. Search for Meaning
2. Be Selfish
3. Be Healthy
4. Make Decisions
5. Be Productive
6. Think Macro
7. Embrace Minimalism
8. Create Value
9. Build Relationships
10. Have Fun

Both lists are deliberately short. Why? Because it's easier to remember. Rest assured, there's still plenty of thought behind them. Here are the extended versions:

Values

I am my own leader

I should always think for myself. This doesn't mean I can't follow others, or be part of a team, or be compassionate. It just means I need to be conscious and deliberate in my decisions—not just floating through life.

I am passionate about my endeavors

I should always seek passion and purpose. If I find myself doing something for other reasons alone (money, fame, power), I should stop and do something else.[87]

I value quality

I don't want to settle. I want to be proud of what I do, proud of what I say, and proud of what I believe in. For that to happen, I must consciously seek great quality in everything I do, and have an opinion about what constitutes great quality.

I am explorative

I should always be curious, seek to learn more, and try new things. I should reflect on my experiences. Otherwise, I'm not growing.

---

87 This doesn't mean I can't do things for money, fame, and power, it just means passion should always be the fundamental force.

I am innovative

I should question the current state of things and seek to build upon, improve, or reinvent them.

I communicate with honesty

Communication is the crux of the social world. I need to be open and honest, even when it's hard. Honesty contributes to my integrity, my character, and my reputation.

I am caring

I'm not alone in the world. I need to respect other's feelings, listen, and practice compassion as much as possible. Understanding others helps us understand ourselves.

I am respectful

I should respect others, without prejudice. Everyone has their own story, their own battles, and their own triumphs. Unconditional respect encourages reciprocation.

I am confident, but humble

Without confidence, this world would swallow me whole, but it's equally important to stay humble (see *I am caring* and *I am respectful*).

I stay grounded

Life is full of peaks and valleys. There will be obstacles, successes, and failures. I should stay calm, enjoy myself, and realize that life is just a series of experiments. The purpose is to enjoy the ride.

Habits

Search for Meaning

I should search for meaning in everything I do. It should be meaningful to *me*. It doesn't really matter what others think.

Be Selfish

I should live life with my best interest in mind. I should not be selfish at the expense of others, but I should also not be selfless at the expense of myself.

Be Healthy

Without health, I have nothing. I must make health a priority so I can excel everywhere else.

Make Decisions

I *must* make decisions. I shouldn't let decisions paralyze me. I don't want to be a passenger in my own life. I want to be the driver.

Be Productive

It's okay to be lazy every now and then, but I should strive for productivity. When I look back at my life, I'll be happier for it.

Think Macro

Don't get caught up in the details. Sometimes a bad day or a failed project can seem like the end of the world, but it's not. Life is a long arc, not a single dot on a line.

Embrace Minimalism

Our society often forces unnecessary things upon us. Stripping it all away reveals clarity, simplicity, and beauty. Most of the time, less is more.

Create Value

I should strive to create value. I want to add substance to this world, not erode it.

Build Relationships

Relationships are an integral part of life. We're social beings. We're not meant to live in a vacuum. With every new relationship, my life is enriched. I'm not talking about Twitter followers and Facebook friends, I'm talking about deep connections that shape both myself and the other person. I should favor the acquisition of friends and experiences over the acquisition of material things.

Have Fun

Life isn't a race. There is no finish line in the distance. I don't know when my journey will end, so all I can do is enjoy it *right now*. I should accept my failures and celebrate my successes. Through it all, I should do my best to appreciate my surroundings, breathe deeply, and have fun.

These lists guide my behavior and keep me focused on what's truly important *to me*. Feel free to use them in your own life, or modify them as you see fit. Self-doubt, attitude problems, toxic relationships, and inspirational roadblocks, can all be confronted more effectively with a solid base of values to guide your actions. Whenever I'm feeling lost, I revisit these lists. Usually, after reading them, I feel centered again.[88]

One Vote of Confidence

Living by the principles of the Connection Algorithm can be daunting. When we push our limits, we invite the possibility of failure into our lives. On the other hand, if we stay in ZombieLand, we risk perpetual unfulfillment. Life is tough either way, and I've experienced depression from both sides. Whenever I'm hit with something particularly negative (a lost loved one, a massive failure at work or in my personal life, a failed relationship, etc.), I often feel like the value of living drops to zero. Time eventually heals, but it can take a *long* time—sometimes years. Luckily, I've found a catalyst that significantly speeds up the process: Genuine support from a non-family member whom you admire and trust.

When I lost my position as the cofounder of my company, I was devastated. Thankfully, after my meltdown, I got a vote of confidence from Brad Feld. It was a thirty second phone conversation, but it turned everything around. My fear turned to confidence. My tenseness faded into relaxation. A calmness-of-mind washed over me, and I suddenly

---

88 I should note that I fail at upholding these values and habits on occasion. It's inevitable. When this happens, I try to admit it to myself and correct it as quickly as possible. It's hard, but worth the effort. Defining your values will help you realize when you've deviated from them, which is why this exercise is so important.

knew that I had the power to be happy, to make a difference, and to simply *live*.

Brad had no idea how much of an impact that thirty-second call had on me. He was just being supportive and positive. So, if you're down in the dumps, find one person you respect and get one vote of confidence. It will make all the difference. Family doesn't count. It needs to be someone who can give you objective support (as opposed to unconditional support, which is essentially *required* from your family). And if you're on the other side of the equation, with the power to breathe confidence into another—do it. It only takes thirty seconds.

Attitude of Gratitude

I heard a great quote the other day from The Minimalists: "Always remember to *love people*, and to *use things*, because doing the opposite never works." It's important to remember that people aren't resources—they're people. You should be grateful and thankful to everyone who supports you.

There's a growing trend within the mentorship community, especially within the startup ecosystem, to give support without expecting anything in return. What an amazing time to be an entrepreneur! The barriers to starting a company (or any other type of project) are lower than ever, and the support system is growing stronger by the day. You can facilitate this ecosystem by being genuinely and unconditionally grateful to the people supporting you. Your gratitude is the fuel that keeps the system running. It's all the payback a mentor ever needs.

Be Honest

Connectors are people, just like you. They're usually more compassionate than most, because they've doubted themselves, been through failure, and felt stressed and depressed beyond belief, just like you. It's hard to tell people how you feel when you feel like shit. Will they judge you? Will they think less of you? Almost always, the answer is no.

You may find yourself in difficult situations when talking to cofounders, partners, or investors. Showing weakness seems like the wrong thing to do, especially when people have placed their trust in you, or invested a bunch of money in you. My recommendation is to tell them how you feel. If you can't bring yourself to do it, get an executive or leadership coach. You need to express yourself. Letting your issues fester is a recipe for disaster, probably in the not-so-distant future.

In the executive coaching arena, there's one name I hear over and over again: Jerry Colonna. I haven't met him in person, but we've exchanged emails, and I've learned a lot about him through his blog, *The Monster in Your Head*.[89] He's a good friend of Brad Feld, and previously worked closely with Fred Wilson, one of the most well-known VCs on the planet. If you need someone to talk to, I recommend giving Jerry a call.

---

89   http://www.themonsterinyourhead.com/

Be a Sponge

Listening to a Connector is better than speaking to one. Connectors usually have an extremely valuable perspective. They've probably been through more shit-storms than you. People talk about the value of experience all the time, but inexperienced people have difficulty believing it because they're inexperienced. It's an incredibly aggravating paradox.

My best advice is to keep your mouth shut. Listen to the people who've already done *it*, whatever *it* is. Soak up their knowledge like a sponge. If there's one thing I learned at my startup, it's that whatever you think is right is probably wrong. First-timers stumble through everything. So, the best way to learn is to listen to the people who've already stumbled. They'll give you advice that sounds completely backwards, which is why you need to listen. The right thing is often counterintuitive. If you listen, you'll still stumble—but you'll stumble less.

Deep Connections

"You are the average of the five people you spend the most time with."

JIM ROHN

Choose your deep connections wisely. Deep connections are the bonds that shape us. It's more beneficial to have a small number of deep connections than a large number of shallow ones.

The best athletes are said to make the rest of their teammates better. But this isn't what makes a star athlete good. It's the *effect* of them being good. The other players on the team become better because they're motivated by the star player. They become better because the star player is adept at involving everyone. They become better because when the opponent is forced to focus on the star, things become easier for everyone else. They become better because the star player is a good teacher. They become better because the star player pushes the level of competition in practice and during the game. They become better because the star can overcome mistakes and get the team back into a winning position. They become better because when the star has faith in them, they begin to have faith in themselves.

If you're part of a winning team, you're winning. It's nearly impossible to experience life in a vacuum, so you might as well surround yourself with greatness. The star players will lift you up without trying. They can't help it. It's what they do.

It's impossible to have deep connections with everyone. The more connections you make, the harder they are to maintain. So don't try to make every connection a deep one. Give priority to your naturally deep connections and allow the rest to be shallow. Shallow connections are still valuable, but don't let them distract you from the few who matter most. When you're falling into the abyss, it's better to have one friend who can pull you out, than 100 friends who will wave goodbye.

Connector Qualities

- David Cohen
- Brad Feld
- Tim Ferriss
- Leo Babauta
- Tony Horton

The Connectors above have helped me tremendously over the years, providing consistent inspiration and—in many cases—direct support. Interestingly, most of them are completely unaware of the impact they've had on my life. While I know David and Brad well, I've only spoken to Tony briefly, and I've never met Tim or Leo. Keep in mind—you don't necessarily need to know a Connector personally to draw inspiration from them. Here's a quick look at some of my favorite Connectors, and what makes them so special.

David Cohen

David is the founder and CEO of TechStars. He also controls two private seed-equity funds and sits on the board of several privately held companies. He's become a force in the Boulder tech community and is known nationally as a savvy and seasoned investor.

I met David when he was just getting TechStars off the ground. He already had a few startups under his belt by that time, but TechStars was completely unproven. When creating TechStars, David took a chance by reaching out to Brad Feld to pitch his idea. Brad loved the concept and joined as a cofounder.

I've watched TechStars expand over the years. It has been an impressive display of consistent growth and success. I feel a sense of pride as a graduate of the inaugural class. Having gone through the process of building a startup myself, I also have tremendous respect for David. In our interactions, I've noticed he's always calm and level-headed. He has a soft toned voice and a humble confidence. He isn't overly talkative, so whenever he speaks, he's usually saying something of value.

David has an eye for talent, and an ability to attract that talent. This is one of his most distinguishing qualities. Convincing Brad to join TechStars was just the tip of the iceberg. He has also built an amazing team at his headquarters in Colorado, and assembled additional programs that operate independently throughout the country and the world. TechStars has become an empire. I believe David's ability to attract smart people is largely a natural gift, but—by some measure—it's also a craft. His aura of calmness and confidence appeals to like-minded people.

The last time I met with David, he was wearing a hooded sweatshirt, jeans, and a pair of stylish, framed glasses. He had a glow in his eyes. He walks with a little more swagger now, although he probably doesn't realize it. I could tell things were going well for him. Sitting across the table from David, I couldn't help but marvel at the mogul he's become. My gut tells me he's in his prime. I have no doubt that his empire will continue to grow.

Brad Feld

Brad is the managing director and founder of Foundry Group, one of the most respected venture capital firms in the country. He lives in Boulder, Colorado, and is arguably the most powerful VC between the coasts. While Brad is commonly known as an investor, he's also a marathon runner, an avid reader, and a prolific writer. He maintains a popular blog called *Feld Thoughts*, where he writes about venture capital, startups, and various personal interests. He has also published several books that cover similar topics.

Brad is one of my biggest idols, and a fantastic friend. I first met him when I joined TechStars in 2007. From the moment I heard him speak, I knew I wanted to make a connection. I remember being on the verge of tears as he explained the magic of entrepreneurship and the opportunity we all had in front of us. I made sure to speak with him afterwards. I approached him, introduced myself, and told him how excited I was to be in the program. He smiled, and said he was excited too. What caught me off guard was how unmistakably genuine he was in his response. I was a young kid, a nobody—yet Brad was glowing with excitement and interest. He was fully engaged.

Brad is one of the most honest people I know. He speaks and writes openly about his successes *and* failures. Throughout his career, he's been particularly transparent with regard to his battles with depression. Seeing a highly successful person communicate with such honesty, humility, and vulnerability, is powerful. It shows Brad's character and lets everyone know that even superheroes have chinks in their armor. This type of introspective honesty is a gift to the entrepreneurial community.

Having a person like Brad in my life continues to be a blessing. He's been a huge inspiration for me. He speaks from his heart, he cares about people, and he's amazing at what he does. He's the archetype of a Connector.

Tim Ferriss

Tim is a best-selling author, entrepreneur, and investor. He graduated from Princeton, started a company, sold it, and then wrote one of the best-selling books of all time, *The Four Hour Workweek*. He has since gone on to write other bestsellers, including *The Four Hour Body*, and *The Four Hour Chef*. His accomplishments beyond this are almost too great to count: He speaks six languages (so far), holds a title as a kickboxing champion in China, and placed in the semi-finals of the Tango World Championship in Buenos Aires—just to name a few. He considers himself a human guinea pig, testing his abilities in a range of disciplines.

Tim's acclaimed bestseller, *The Four Hour Workweek*, is the book you should read next. If you've already read it, read it again. It's that good. While my book may equip you with the necessary mindset to do big things and give you the tools to get started—Tim's book digs much deeper into the nitty gritty of it all. It's an amazing resource.

Tim has an authentic voice. In all the research I've done on him, this is the quality that stands out the most. Of course he is acutely intelligent, but his ability to communicate naturally and effectively is what sets him apart from other thought leaders. It makes perfect sense. Tim has dedicated his life to simplifying the world around him. He finds ways to cut the fat and get straight to the meat. Regardless of what he's learning about, that's always his approach. So naturally, it flows into his writing and teaching styles, too.

One of the best things about Tim is his propensity for sharing. He shares his knowledge, but also the knowledge of others. His blog is one of the most powerful platforms in the world, and he constantly allows friends and colleagues to share their ideas there. I presume Tim does this because he understands the importance of *value*. Value is all that matters. He isn't caught up in serving only himself. He is instead focused on providing value to everyone else around him, including other visionaries, and—most importantly— his audience. He knows it's not a zero sum game. Everybody can win.

Tim is brilliant in so many ways. When I look at his achievements, I think to myself *"He gets it."* Business, marketing, relationships, happiness, success, life. He "gets" all of it.

Leo Babauta

Leo is a writer. Originally from Guam, he now lives in San Francisco with his wife and six children. In 2005, Leo was freelancing and unable to support his family. He was addicted to smoking, overweight, unhealthy, and unhappy.

Then things changed.

Leo quit smoking. He became an avid runner, running half-marathons, marathons, and ultramarathons (fifty miles). He even conquered a triathlon. He became a vegetarian, and then a vegan, shedding sixty-five pounds of fat. He also started a blog called *Zen Habits*, which became one of the most trafficked blogs on the internet. It has over one million monthly subscribers as of this writing. He followed this up with several books. Then he created his own membership program called the Sea Change Program, which helps people change their habits and live better lives.

Throughout all of this, Leo gradually simplified his lifestyle. He completely eliminated his debt, became financially independent, and saved up a huge emergency fund. He cleared the clutter from his life, keeping only what was necessary.

Leo's transformation and subsequent achievements have been jaw-dropping. He lives through passion and passion only, which has afforded him the life he wants. Interestingly, he doesn't follow rules or conventions. Instead, he decides what's best for him and the people he serves. Then, he executes on it relentlessly. You won't find any ads on Leo's blog. Why? Because ads are annoying. They're a distraction, and don't provide much value to the reader. Just because everyone else is doing it doesn't make it the only solution.

All of Leo's work is uncopyrighted. Why? Because—why not? Without a copyright, anyone can take Leo's content and paste it wherever they please. Leo doesn't mind. It only helps spread his message, which is exactly what he wants. Why would he copyright his work and force people to jump through hoops to share it?

Leo offers the material on his blog (and some of his ebooks) for free. He shares his knowledge because he knows he'll be paid back in other ways. Since 2005, Leo hasn't had a job. He funds his life by doing what he loves—thinking, dreaming, running, and writing. Leo touches a million people's lives every month, including mine. I'd say he's a bit of a Connector. From Leo's blog:

So you're reading some of my posts on how to achieve your goals, and how to save money or exercise or wake up early, and you're wondering…what exactly are my qualifications?

My answer is that I have no formal qualifications. I am not an expert, or a doctor, or a coach. I haven't made millions of dollars and I'm not the world's greatest athlete.

All I am is a regular guy, a father of six kids, a husband, a writer from Guam (now living in San Francisco). But I have accomplished a lot over the last couple of years (and failed a lot) and along the way, I have learned a lot.[90]

Although Leo has overcome so many obstacles, he humbly admits that he has far more to learn. He is truly a student of the earth and is likely one of the kindest people you could ever meet, if his writing is any indication. Although his achievements are astonishing, he isn't superhuman. He just lives the life of a Connector.

If you haven't done so, check out his blog, *Zen Habits*: http://zenhabits.net/. Not only is the content fantastic, but the entire philosophy of the blog is in line with the principles of the Connection Algorithm, in terms of building products, connecting with people, and generally being in control of your life. I found Leo's blog when I was in the midst of a deep depression. His words were instrumental in bringing me out of the shadows. Thank you, Leo.

---

90 http://zenhabits.net/my-story/

Tony Horton

Tony is the host and creator of P90X, one of the most successful workout DVD programs ever created. Tony has also produced a range of other DVD programs including Power 90, Power Half Hour, 10 Minute Trainer, P90X One-on-One, P90X2, and P90X3, among others. Tony has trained a long list of celebrities, including Tom Petty, Billy Idol, Lindsey Buckingham, Stevie Nicks, Shirley MacLaine, Sean Connery, Annie Lennox, Rob Lowe, Antonio Banderas, Bruce Springsteen, Usher, and Ewan McGregor. He has also appeared on The Dr. Oz Show and several other popular TV programs.[91]

One of Tony's best attributes is his casual nature. He's extremely likable. In his early days, he considered becoming an actor, and even spent a short time working as a standup comic. His love of the stage paid off in the fitness world. Throughout the P90X DVD series (and all of his other videos), Tony makes jokes and pokes fun at himself. He immediately forms a connection with his audience through casual commentary, which makes his programs light-hearted and fun. Tony also has an incredibly positive attitude. He's slow to praise himself and quick to praise others.

His *best* attribute, though, is his passion. He's genuinely excited when his pupils get results. There's an infomercial for the most recent installment of P90X. My favorite part is when Tony tears up. He's talking about people who struggled with their health in the past, but found a way to make progress with P90X3. He literally starts crying in the middle of the commercial. Clearly, it wasn't planned. It was just

---

91   http://tinyurl.com/42xb2m5

Tony being Tony. He's truly passionate about his craft, and it shows.

Tony got to where he is today because he followed the principles of the Connection Algorithm to a tee. He used the Four Cs: Choose, Commit, Create, Connect. He *chose* to take a risk by following his passion for acting and comedy. Instead of graduating from college, he moved to California with almost no money. In an attempt to score more acting gigs, he began exercising, and then became a professional trainer after finding success with it. (i.e. He found a lucrative Purpose Spurt and latched on). As his passion revealed itself, he *committed* to it 100%. He *created* highly addictive and effective workout routines, which helped him *connect* with high-profile clients. That success then caught the eye of Beachbody, the company that distributes P90X.

Things weren't always perfect for Tony. He experienced plenty of failure. When he first moved to California to become an actor, he could barely pay for food. He even performed as a mime on the Santa Monica pier. Can you imagine? Tony Horton, the famous fitness star, escaping from an imaginary box and asking for tips? That's the reality of finding true success. It requires grit, sacrifice, and determination. It's not always smooth, and it's not always pretty.

It's amazing how this process reveals itself over and over again. It's the story of every successful Connector I've ever studied, and it's no coincidence. It's simply the Connection Algorithm in action.

Being a Connector

Are you a Connector, or on your way to becoming one? If so, this section will teach you how to be the best Connector you can be. Here's the shortlist of what you need to do:

- Connect People
- Get 'Em While They're Young
- Support Apprenticeship
- Expect Nothing in Return
- Create Value
- Remember Where You Came From

Connect People

When you become an expert in your field, you'll be seen as an influencer. People may reach out to you for introductions to others. If you can make these introductions without much hassle, do it. The more people you can support, the better. That said, don't spread yourself too thin either, or you'll burn out—like an entrepreneur without focus.

Get 'Em While They're Young

Young people are more impressionable and able to adapt. They have less holding them back, little to lose, and everything to gain. It's easier to mold young people into capable passion-seekers, before obstacles like fear and self-doubt set in. For all of you parents out there, you're clearly in a prime position to get 'em while they're young. Give your little ones the courage to dream big. Push them. Let them fall. Then prop them back up.

Support Apprenticeship

Ben Franklin, Vincent van Gogh, and Henry Ford—they were all apprentices before they accomplished their best work. They gained knowledge from family members, friends, and colleagues. If you have the opportunity to mentor a promising individual closely, you should see it as a gift. While it may be a significant commitment, it will also be rewarding. Be picky. This person must be special. She needs the capacity—with your direction—to possess all of the qualities described in this book: the willingness to take risks, relentless persistence and determination, the ability to create something meaningful from nothing, and a true appreciation for the value of relationships.

Expect Nothing in Return

When people become excessively wealthy, they often donate to charities. When a donation is made, the donor doesn't expect anything in return, except for maybe an acknowledgment of some kind. The donor understands she is giving simply to give.

For some reason, giving unconditionally is far less common when it comes to business and mentorship. Investors and advisors typically ask for a board seat, or a percentage of equity, in exchange for their expertise. If you're an investor, this should *not* be your approach 100% of the time. On occasion, you should donate your time and wisdom for free. This is one of the few ways to connect the less-connected. You'll be rewarded with self-fulfillment and, who knows—maybe you'll launch the next Richard Branson to the moon.

Create Value

Create value whenever possible. You may have access to resources that can propel a person's career forward. Spreading your wisdom through speaking engagements or the written word can also be beneficial. Even your casual advice and encouragement is worth more than you know. The best Connectors make a difference in people's lives. They spend time giving back.

Remember Where You Came From

As a Connector, remembering where you came from is mission critical. You weren't always as fortunate as you are now. At a point in your past, you were still developing your skills, meeting new people, and exploring the world. Then somebody came along and set your life on a new trajectory that contributed to who you are today.

There are countless young people (and adults) who are just like the younger, less successful version of you. They're hungry to grow, and hungry to learn. They haven't fully bloomed yet, but they're ready and willing to become the best versions of themselves. Some of these people will become great leaders, influential thinkers, inventors, scientists, writers, artists, and CEOs. But they need your help. They need the extra push, the extra confidence, the extra inspiration to overcome the intense battles and setbacks that they will inevitably face. Offering your support in just one of these battles could be the spark that turns self-doubt into self-confidence.

The more we acknowledge the importance of enabling these new stars to rise, the stronger our society will be. We need to give people permission to challenge the status quo, aim high, and risk failure. The power to shape the leaders of tomorrow rests in your hands. Don't let that power go to waste.

FINAL THOUGHTS

"That day, for no particular reason, I decided to go for a little run. So I ran to the end of the road. And when I got there, I thought maybe I'd run to the end of town. And when I got there, I thought maybe I'd just run across Greenbow County. And I figured, since I run this far, maybe I'd just run across the great state of Alabama. And that's what I did. I ran clear across Alabama. For no particular reason I just kept on going. I ran clear to the ocean. And when I got there, I figured, since I'd gone this far, I might as well turn around, just keep on going. When I got to another ocean, I figured, since I'd gone this far, I might as well just turn back, keep right on going."

FORREST, *FORREST GUMP*

The Connection Algorithm was inspired by a blog post. To date, it's my most popular story—by a mile. When I wrote that post, there was no plan. I had no idea it would eventually turn into a book. I was just writing because I felt like writing. It seemed fitting to end this book with the post that started it, so here it is:

Be Like Nike: Just Do It!

I've done it. I've discovered the secret to prolonged happiness. Yes, it's taken me thirty years and I still have to remind myself constantly, but I've figured it out. Ready? Here it is—the secret to being happy:

Do shit you like to do.

Okay, I know this is stupidly obvious. But sometimes the most obvious truths are the most elusive and overlooked.

We usually discover our passions by following our joy. Whether it's writing, or watching movies, or building products, or fishing, or drawing, or solving algebraic equations, we tend to explore various activities and then latch on to the ones we like the most. But then somewhere along the journey of growing up, we get sucked into schoolwork and resumes and bills and jobs and mortgages. Before we get a chance to take a breath, we realize we can't do the things we like to do anymore. We're stuck. Such is life, right? *Wrong!*

Stop assuming your life is on a prescribed trajectory—this is the opposite of reality. You are always in control. When I look back at my life, I realize the most positive and important decisions I've made have come from being almost idiotically risky and deliberate when I knew I wanted to change something. In these scenarios, I went after something new without considering the challenges or consequences that might arise from it. Whether it was a girl, a job, a hobby, a new friend—I just went for it. You have to do this. You have to stop thinking so much and *go and get it*. There are plenty of things that can keep you happy, but you have to seek them out.

There's a quote on my desk on a small scrap of paper:

> "I finally figured out the only reason
> to be alive is to enjoy it."
>
> RITA MAE BROWN

I need to constantly remind myself of this, which is why I leave the quote on my desk. It's also the only quote on my desk. Honestly, what else is there to remember?

I've spent periods of my life—long periods, waiting for things to happen because I thought something was at the end of the tunnel. Guess what? There was nothing at the end of the tunnel because life isn't a tunnel. Life is an open field. With each moment, we can decide to do anything we want. There isn't a finite end to the path we're on. In fact, there isn't a path at all. The only sure thing waiting for us, despite the direction we take, is death. Stop telling yourself you're on a path. You're not. You're only in a distinct moment, and the next moment can take you in any direction you choose. It's a scary truth, but it's liberating.

We tend to force ourselves into corners and trick ourselves into thinking we're not good enough, not smart enough, not determined enough, too old, too young, too tired, too weak. Or we tell ourselves we're already on a path to something good and that we'll get there eventually. It's all BS. We conjure up these thoughts because we're too scared to figure out if any of it is true or not.

I wanted to write for a long time, but felt I shouldn't do it because people in my social and professional circles might not like it or might judge me in some way. It took a life-changing event for me to finally get the nerve to start writing publicly. Now that I'm doing it, it feels amazing. It's like crack. I become energized thinking about what I might write next and how I can connect with an audience. The happiness I've gained from writing is well worth any negative consequence that may come from it. My nervousness in getting started was a barrier created from my own self-doubt.

The simple truth is that *there is no reason not to do what you love.* Whatever obstacle you have in your head is bullshit. You've fabricated it out of thin air because you're nervous. Don't have time? BS. Make time. Seriously, watch one less TV show. Doesn't pay the bills? BS. First of all, you can do what you love outside of work if you make time (see above). Second, you can usually pay the bills doing something you love—you just have to be creative, persistent, and go all in. Family members or friends don't support it? BS. It's not their choice, it's yours. Reconsider who you're spending time with if they're not supporting you. Sometimes people think they're helping you because they foresee a potential obstacle in what you plan to do, don't think it's worthwhile, or doubt your ability. These are the same internal fears you have, reinforced by others. *Run!* It's only compounding the issue and digging you into a deeper hole of indecision.

All of these forces against us are hard to overcome. Believe me, I know. But, plain and simple—overcoming them is worth it. It took me over thirty years to realize this, but it's true. Would you rather be perpetually sad to avoid potentially negative consequences that probably won't ever materialize, or would you rather vastly increase your likelihood of being perpetually happy? When you look at it from this perspective, the choice is obvious. It's a risk we should all take.

So, do yourself a favor and start enjoying yourself. Do the thing you're most scared of doing—the thing you've always wanted to do. Remove all obstacles. End the relationship. Quit the job. Enroll in the class you've been wanting to take. Spend your nights learning a new craft instead of watching TV. And don't trick yourself into liking something you don't. Do you really like eating fatty foods to the detriment of your health? Do you really like your current job, or are you just doing it as a means to an end? Think critically about these types of things. It's easy to fool yourself.

Remember, the only reason to be alive is to enjoy it. I don't care what you enjoy doing—it's your life. I care that you stop thinking about it and start taking action. Be like Nike. *Just do it*. You'll be glad you did.

LET'S MAKE IT FLY

Hey there! I owe you, (yes *you*—holding this book) a huge "Thank you." *The Connection Algorithm* has become a #1 bestseller in multiple categories on Amazon, including Entrepreneurship, Management, Knowledge Capital, and Personal Success. The book's message is resonating with people throughout the country, and *the world*.

This book is completely self-published. That means there's not a big, powerful publishing company promoting it. Readers like *you* are supporting and funding its growth. I'd be forever grateful if you continued your support by posting an honest review on Amazon. Here's the link:

http://tinyurl.com/qa4ycsw

You can also simply search for: "*The Connection Algorithm Amazon*" on Google, and the link to the Amazon page will pop right up. Once you're there, just scroll down and click the button that says: "Write a customer review." From there, you'll be able to leave your thoughts, including your expectations when you first opened the book, your perspective on specific chapters, and what you took away from it in general. Feel free to express your true feelings (positive *or* negative).

The most effective tools for marketing and distributing products now rest rightfully in the hands of the consumer. *You,* sitting in that chair, have the power to push *The Connection Algorithm's* message forward, or let it fade. Please help it reach the top ranks of Amazon so more people can discover it. And if you want to reach out to me personally for any reason, feel free to email me at jesse.tevelow@gmail.com, or tweet me @jtevelow.

Forever grateful, J

ACKNOWLEDGMENTS

There are so many people to thank. First and foremost, I need to thank my parents. Mom and Dad, you've helped me become the person I am today. I spent over a year of my life unemployed, putting this book together, and you never pushed me to get a real job. Not once. You supported me the whole way. Your acceptance and support of my constant risk-taking might be the biggest reason that I've experienced the Connection Algorithm firsthand. And for that, I thank you both from the bottom of my heart.

Ben and Rachel (and little Owen), Nora, Kristy, Hayley, and Kevin—thank you for being so supportive. I'm blessed to have all of you in my life.

To Joe and Ryan, thank you for taking me on such a wild ride, and for dealing with my younger, unenlightened self for so many years. I'll always respect you guys. You're both brilliant, and I feel privileged to have worked with you.

David and Brad, it's impossible to connect the dots looking forward, but I can definitely connect them looking back. You both changed my life in 2007, and the advice and opportunities you've given me since then have been incredible. With the success you've both had, I don't understand how you even find time to speak with me, yet you provide meaningful support over and over and over again. I am forever grateful to have you both in my corner. I consider you as mentors, but more importantly, as friends.

To Simon and Lily, Matt and Julia, Robyn and Chad, and Tori—thank you for being my support group and my local crew as I worked on this project. Simon, you kept me motivated. Bouncing ideas off of you was always helpful. Matt, sometimes I wasn't sure if I needed a real editor with your brilliant insights and thoughtful comments keeping me in line. Thank you, all of you, for letting me sleep on your couches when I was low on cash. And thank you AirBNB, for allowing me to make money while I slept on other people's couches.

To Casey, as a fellow writer and one of my best longtime friends, I respect your opinion more than you know. Thank you for taking the time to help me turn my jumbled thoughts into coherent prose. To Kel, thank you for the constant support and positivity, even though you always interrupt me while I'm eating. To Zach, my best bud, thanks for the encouragement from afar and for helping with the Kickstarter campaign. Thank you to Andrew Grove, for your unexpected donation, and to Darrell Brookstein, Founder & CEO of Spexio, Inc., for your generosity and patience.

To my family members and friends who read early drafts of the book, thank you. Even if you didn't provide feedback, putting the draft into people's hands gave me the drive to continuously improve it. Donna Fenn, thank you for acting as my impromptu mentor for this project. PJ Russ, thanks for making me look so good (is that really me?). Adam Patch and Alexander Brandon, you guys are rockstars. Thanks for putting together a killer brand and top-notch promotional materials. I get pumped every time I watch the trailer. You really nailed it. Sarah Lingley, thank you for the much needed copy edit. Michelle and Dan, thank you for getting the book into it's final form. Everyone on the production team—you all live through your passions, as is evidenced by your amazing work (so...I guess you don't need to read the book)!

To all of the Connectors I've mentioned: 37Signals, Alexis Ohanian, Andy Dunn, Bart Lorang, Ben Horowitz, Brad Feld, David Cohen, Elon Musk, Eric Ries, Floyd Mayweather, Gary Vaynerchuk, Joe Aigboboh, Leo Babauta, Malcolm Gladwell, Marcus Kleiewer, Mark Zuckerberg, Matt Galligan, Meng To, Naveen Selvadurai, Ryan Komori, Seth Godin, Stewart Butterfield, The Minimalists, Tim Ferriss, Tony Horton, Tyler Ward, Wiley Cerilli—thank you for being the trailblazers and passion-seekers that you are. You unknowingly provided me with the blueprint and the inspiration to write this book. I will continue to look in your direction for wisdom and motivation.

Tony, reading *The Big Picture* helped me put the finishing touches on my manuscript, and chatting with you affected me more than you know. It validated my entire thesis. It proved that the Connection Algorithm really works.

You've helped me transform my body, but also my mind and my soul. Thank you for teaching me to always do my best, forget the rest, and "bring it."

Finally, I'd like to thank *you*, the reader. None of this would mean anything without you. Thank you for taking the risk of reading this book. It was a shallow risk, but you still took it, and I'm grateful for that. Hopefully you are, too. Now get out there, and start making moves.

If you enjoyed this book, or just want to reach out,
Tweet at me: @jtevelow

INDEX

ABOUT THE AUTHOR

Jesse Warren Tevelow is an entrepreneur and writer. He cofounded PlayQ Inc., and was a member of the inaugural class of TechStars. Earlier in his career, Jesse worked for Seamless (acquired by Aramark in 2006) and Keynote Systems. Jesse has been featured in various publications, including *Businessweek Magazine*, *Do More Faster* (by Brad Feld and David Cohen), and *Upstarts* (by Donna Fenn). *The Connection Algorithm* is Jesse's first book. To find out more, go to www.jtev.me

95299264R00143

Made in the USA
Lexington, KY
07 August 2018